T odd stood and brushed off his jeans. "I'm okay, really," he said with an apologetic shrug. "Let's play ball."

Kate waited until the team began to return to their positions before she spoke. "I had better," she said, her lungs burning with barely restrained emotion, "see you batting, fielding, and sliding through the dirt in the next two innings."

His dark eyes blazed, but he didn't speak.

"Or else," she continued, trying to come up with a threat that would mean anything to Todd.

He gave her a cocky grin that didn't quite reach his eyes, as if daring her with her words. *Or else, what?* his gaze seemed to ask.

Her mind drew a blank. "Or else," she concluded lamely, the fire extinguished from her tone.

"I'll play ball the way you want," he said, his voice low and controlled.

She'd obviously made him angry. Well, so be it. If he felt he couldn't play a stupid softball game because he might hurt her feelings, then he didn't know her very well. The thought struck her that before she'd met Todd, her feelings *would* have been hurt by such an action. He'd been the one to help her rise above those feelings, get beyond her fear, but he wasn't giving her a chance to prove it.

He wasn't finished. "If you promise you'll have dinner with me, no matter what happens. Deal?"

Kate met Todd stare for stare, noticing with some relief that the familiar twinkle of laughter was back in his gaze.

"Deal," she said finally, tugging the brow of her cap down over her eyes. "Now, let's play ball!"

D0190806

A PALISADES CONTEMPORARY ROMANCE

Beloved

Debra Kastner

PALISADES

PALISADES IS A DIVISION OF MULTNOMAH PUBLISHERS, INC.

This is a work of fiction. The characters, incidents, and dialogues are products of
the author's imagination and are not to be construed as real. Any resemblance to
actual events or persons, living or dead, is entirely coincidental.

BELOVED
published by Palisades
a division of Multnomah Publishers, Inc.

© 1998 by Debra Kastner
International Standard Book Number: 1–57673–331-9

Cover illustration by Dan Brown/Artworks, Inc.
Design by Brenda McGee

Most Scripture quotations are from:
The Holy Bible, King James Version

Palisades is a trademark of Multnomah Publishers, Inc.,
and is registered in the U.S. Patent and Trademark Office.

Printed in the United States of America

ALL RIGHTS RESERVED
No part of this publication may be reproduced, stored in a retrieval system, or
transmitted, in any form or by any means—electronic, mechanical, photocopying,
recording, or otherwise—without prior written permission.

For information:
MULTNOMAH PUBLISHERS, INC.
POST OFFICE BOX 1720
SISTERS, OREGON 97759

Library of Congress Cataloging-in-Publication Data:
Kastner, Deb.
Beloved / by Debra Kastner.
p. cm.
ISBN 1–57673–331-9
I. Title.
PS3561.A724B4 1998
813'.54—dc21   98–688
                                                        CIP

98 99 00 01 02 03 04 — 10 9 8 7 6 5 4 3 2 1

To my own most beloved,
my husband and my best friend,
Joseph C. Kastner Jr.

One

WANTED: Part-time Christian pastor with a full-time heart to perform wedding ceremonies at a lovely Colorado-mountain chapel location. Team player needed to work closely with wedding coordinator. Come join this growing ministry!

Kate Logan shuffled the papers before her and sighed wearily. Oblivious to the muted chatter of the surrounding coffeehouse patrons, she blew a wisp of dismally straight, chestnut brown hair from her eyes and squinted at the next name on her list.

Father Todd Jensen.

A quick glance at her watch confirmed she had five minutes to spare. She leaned her head back on the glaring red vinyl booth and closed her eyes, letting her breath seep slowly from her lungs.

It had been a long morning. She'd had no idea finding a minister to marry people in their little chapel nestled in the foothills of the Rocky Mountains just west of Denver would be so difficult. She considered the opportunity to be a better-than-average part-time job and wasn't surprised by the phenomenal number of responses and inquiries.

When she and her business partners placed the advertisement, Kate had pictured a kind, elderly retired man, or maybe a young intern fresh out of seminary. Instead, she'd been bombarded by inappropriate candidates—everything from a displaced hippie with "Jesus Saves" tie-dyed on his T-shirt to a red-faced evangelist raging hellfire and brimstone through quivering jowls.

Father Todd Jensen.

A nice, sensible name. Her mind conjured a sweet, solemn-faced retired man with a hearing aid in one ear and an endearing propensity for falling asleep at awkward intervals.

Father Todd Jensen. The last name on her list. *Please, God, make this one work out.*

"Kate Logan?" A rich, deep voice penetrated her thoughts and brought her instantly alert.

Her eyes snapped open and locked onto huge, liquid brown eyes laced with humor. Young eyes, complementing a young man's smiling face. Her breath caught in her throat.

"Uh, yes. I beg your pardon," she stammered, coughing to cover her lapse. She mentally berated herself for being caught unaware. She'd worked too hard to be taken so completely off guard. Above all, she wished to look professional.

"Father Todd Jensen. I'm two minutes early. Hope I didn't interrupt your nap."

Her breath left her lungs as if he'd sucker punched her. Surprise must have registered on her face, for his grin widened, exposing a line of slightly crooked teeth—not enough to warrant braces, but enough to give him an endearing smile.

He raised his dark eyebrows. "Not what you expected?"

She shook her head, speechless.

"You thought I'd be…"

"Older," she admitted, feeling the heat rush to her face.

"Older," he repeated, crooking a finger under his chin and nodding in mock seriousness. "Okay. I can do older."

He tossed a well-worn file folder onto the table across from her and retraced his steps to the front of the coffee shop. Ruffling his short-cropped black hair and stooping his broad shoulders, he shuffled slowly back to Kate's table, supporting his shuddering steps with an imaginary cane.

"Father Todd Jensen," he acknowledged in a rusty, old man's voice. "Do I get the job now?"

Despite her reticence, Kate couldn't help but laugh. "You do an excellent older. Perhaps you missed your calling."

He chuckled and slid into the booth opposite her. Despite his muscular build, he looked totally relaxed. "I was an actor in high school." He folded his hands on the table and gave her a direct look that flustered her even more than his handsome face.

Without a doubt, Father Todd was one of the best-looking men Kate had ever seen. He was broad and stocky, his wide shoulders tapering down to a trim waist. *Built like a wrestler,* she thought, *or a baseball player.* The denim shirt he wore did nothing to hide a thick chest and huge biceps.

He certainly had unusual dress for a man of the cloth. A denim shirt capped by a clerical collar? Stonewashed blue jeans held up with purple Colorado Rockies suspenders? Not what she considered a typical pastor. Her mind raced as she tried to gather her thoughts.

The sound of forks clinking on ceramic plates and spoons stirring sugar into coffee cups suddenly seemed to whirl into a huge din. She glanced at Todd's left hand, unconsciously singling out his ring finger. It was bare. But then, didn't priests take a vow of celibacy?

"Are you married?" she blurted, and then blushed to the roots of her hair at her own audacity. Not only could she be slapped with a sexual harassment lawsuit if Father Jensen felt so inclined, but the question was downright rude.

She stammered, trying to cover her error. "I-I mean, I know some of you people can't marry."

"That would be the Roman Catholics," he replied, lifting an eyebrow. "Which I'm not. *We people* like to marry."

He paused and leaned forward, his face inches from hers.

She felt her heartbeat quickening at their forced intimacy but resisted the impulse to pull away.

"To answer your question, I'm not married." His voice softened, and the hint of a smile played on his lips. "Right now, I'm too busy with the ministry to be involved in a serious relationship. But I hope to marry someday. When I find the right woman."

Kate leaned back into the booth and broke eye contact, her emotions a swirling mist of alarm and relief. She had the unnerving feeling that this man whom she had known for all of five minutes was peeling away the armor she'd built around her heart…yet she couldn't deny her satisfaction in knowing he was single.

Not that it mattered. She wasn't interested in men. Not in marrying one, anyway. Marriage was—well, it simply wasn't for her. And the admittedly handsome man sitting across from her wasn't going to change her opinion on that subject.

As if he would want to, she mentally amended, laughing at her own foolishness. She wasn't his type. She wasn't anybody's type. And this man looked like he'd go for a willowy blonde. Something in the cover-model category. To her misfortune, she wasn't willowy or blonde, never mind cover-model material.

Oh, why am I thinking about this, anyway? He's way out of my league, no matter what type of woman he prefers. And he just said he isn't interested in a relationship.

You're interviewing him for a job, for pity's sake. She forced her thoughts back to the business at hand.

"Do you have your résumé, Father? Er—that's how I should address you, isn't it?"

Reminding Kate of a large cat, he stretched back into the booth, locking his hands behind his head. "You may refer to me as Your Most Reverend Holiness, if you'd like."

When Kate's jaw dropped in astonishment, he laughed, a thick, deep rumble from the depths of his chest. "Just Todd, please." He handed her his résumé, encased in the well-used file folder.

"Todd, then," Kate said, recovering. "And I'm glad to meet you."

What was it about this man that threw her off balance? His collar was part of it, to be sure. She'd always found pastors a little intimidating. But she'd been interviewing pastors all day and had nowhere near the fuzz-for-brains reaction she was having to Todd.

She shook herself mentally and glanced down the length of the résumé. "Let me tell you a bit about my company."

He rested his arms across the back of the booth and nodded for her to continue, his attention completely and unnervingly focused on her face.

"I started consulting for weddings purely by accident. When I graduated from college, several of my friends married and asked for my help getting their weddings together. I found I had a real knack for organizing, and information about my services spread by word of mouth."

She tapped her pencil absently against the tabletop. "Soon I had hooked up with several reliable retailers and services and realized, somewhat belatedly, that I was running a business. Wedding Works was born."

Todd nodded.

"We incorporated two years ago. I have two partners, photographer Thomas Quinn and Elizabeth Edwards, who does the bookkeeping. I pretty much cover the rest."

"That sounds like a lot of work."

"Yes, but I enjoy it. Meeting people. Making dreams come

true." Smiling absently, Kate paused and steepled her fingers. "We just invested in the chapel. I noticed how many of the couples I worked with were looking for something small and intimate and couldn't find what they wanted."

"Out of curiosity, why not churches?"

"If a couple shares a home church, that is usually the best option. However, many couples prefer something different for their wedding day. Chapels dedicated just to weddings are few and far between. We took a financial risk, but it's already paying off. We're booked through the first of the year."

"Ah. My kind of company," he teased.

She laughed. "Enough about Wedding Works. Tell me about yourself. Why did you respond to this ad?"

Todd smiled widely. "As you've probably guessed by now, I'm not your typical pastor." He looped a finger through his suspenders and snapped them for emphasis. "My call doesn't include an ordinary parish. I'm here to serve people the rest of the world passes by." His face flushed with color as his eyes took on the shadow of a dreamer.

"Such as?" She found herself holding her breath as she awaited his answer, whether from curiosity or something deeper she couldn't have said.

"I'm currently working part-time in a retirement community. Before that I worked as a hospital chaplain in an AIDS hospice."

"A retirement community and an AIDS hospice? That makes marrying people sound simple. Why do you want this position?"

"Money, for starters. I figure two part-time jobs will equal one whole paycheck."

Kate threw her shoulders back in her seat, seeking the reassurance of the solid vinyl booth. She reached for her Day-

Timer and made a pretense of laying it out flat, using the moment to gather her thoughts.

He was certainly straightforward, she thought, scribbling an incoherent note in the margin of the day's page. The man unnerved her. Dropping her pencil, she moved her hands under the table and clenched them together to keep from shaking.

"Seriously, though," he continued with a wink, "I like a challenge."

"How do you mean?" She didn't consider officiating at wedding ceremonies to be exceptionally challenging. Not compared to being a chaplain at an AIDS hospice.

"When you consider that half of today's marriages end in divorce, I'd say getting people hitched is quite a challenge. Getting them to *stay* hitched is, at any rate."

"And how do you propose to do that?"

Todd's eyes met hers, and she read there a refreshing sincerity of spirit. "If you're looking for someone to perform quickie services, you've got the wrong man. I'd want to do a series of counseling sessions with each couple before the big day. I don't mind marrying two unbelievers, but I better state up front that I won't marry a believer to an unbeliever."

Kate let out the breath she'd been holding with an audible whoosh.

Todd was the first man she'd interviewed who'd mentioned that very important aspect of the wedding ceremony. As she and her partners had outlined it, this was the key qualification for the position. After having a heart for God, that is.

God's love poured from his eyes like a fountain, and she had to respect a man who put aside material ambitions in order to help others. She suddenly wished she had a little more to offer him in the way of a salary, but for now, part-time was the best she could do. And Todd Jensen couldn't commit to full-time anyway, with his other job.

She had found her man. And the loop-de-loops her heart was doing in her chest had nothing whatsoever to do with her decision. Calm and rational, that was Kate Logan.

"You've answered my questions," she said, surprised at how smooth and businesslike her voice sounded. "Are there any you'd like to ask me?"

"Just one."

She smiled for him to continue.

"It's not a make-it-or-break-it question, but it helps to know. Your advertisement said you were looking for a Christian pastor. Is this a Christian business, or do you have other types of chaplains working for you as well?"

"That's a very astute question." Kate nodded. "Elizabeth, Thomas, and I are all committed Christians. Of course, we serve the general public, but we especially enjoy helping Christian couples get a good start to their marriages."

"I'm glad to hear it." He grinned, and she returned the smile.

Kate made up her mind. She stood and extended her hand. "Father Jensen, if you want it, the position is yours."

Todd stood and shook her hand with an enthusiastic grip.

"Can you start Monday morning? We have an office here in town—just two rooms in Thomas's basement. There's a consulting room there that we use to meet with couples. You can use it for your counseling sessions. But I'd like to show you the chapel first, so why don't you meet me there?" She riffled through her Day-Timer and plucked a photocopied map from within. "These are the directions."

He folded the map haphazardly and stuffed it into the pocket of his denim shirt.

Kate cocked an eyebrow at the now wrinkled paper peeking from his pocket. A smile tipped the corner of her lips.

He smiled back, removed the paper and, with a friendly wink, spread it wide, ironing out the wrinkles with the palm of his hand as he followed her out the door to the parking lot.

The job was his! He sat behind the wheel of his truck and silently looked at the map in his hand. A sense of elation and relief flooded his chest.

Up until he saw that ad, he wasn't sure what he was going to do. He couldn't find it in his heart to quit working at Roseborough, not with so many dear folks depending on him. For many of them, he was their only visitor. He couldn't—he wouldn't—let them down. And now he wouldn't have to. He was going to make it. And his sister…

Shaking off the hovering thought, he recalled Kate's pleasantly round face and blunt-cut chestnut hair. Quiet faith glowed in her eyes, and Todd found himself attracted to their amber depths. But something else lurked in her eyes, something that automated Todd's pastoral nature.

Pain.

He knew it with the certainty of a man called by God to help others—Kate Logan was hiding something. Somewhere, deep down, lay a malignant cancer eating away at her soul. He'd seen it before in others he counseled. He felt the familiar, deep inner prompting to reach out to her, to share in her pain.

To protect her.

What was he thinking? He hardly knew the woman. His

seminary education was getting the best of him, he chided himself. If he wasn't careful, he'd start analyzing the check-out clerk when he went to the grocery store. He scrubbed a hand down his face.

Kate Logan was his employer. He might jeopardize his job if he started prying into her private life. And he needed this job.

"Did you hire someone?" Thomas turned from the table where he was sorting photographs and raised his white-blond eyebrows in inquiry.

The office wasn't much to look at, but they didn't bring clients in, so appearance wasn't an issue. One entire wall was lined with paper-laden four-drawer file cabinets of various colors and conditions. They, along with most of the rest of the office furniture, had been purchased used.

Thomas had a table near the back where he worked on his photographs, and he'd built a small darkroom in one corner for developing.

Two well-worn oak desks lined the other side of the room. Kate's desk was neat as a pin, with various in-and-out trays tidily stacked with papers and neatly labeled file folders. A small black notebook computer lay open on one corner.

Elizabeth sat at the other desk amidst piles of ledgers, a calculator, and a random selection of multicolored Post-it notes. She looked up, throwing her waist-length blond hair to one side of her shoulder. "Well, did you?"

"Um, yes. Yes, I did," Kate answered slowly. She was still feeling somewhat dazed from her encounter with Todd.

"So tell us about him!" Elizabeth encouraged.

"He's…" Handsome. Funny. Kind. "Uh…young." She shook her head to dislodge the echo of his vibrant laugh.

"Young. Now that was definitely the first requirement on our list," Elizabeth teased. "From the look on your face, I'm guessing he's nice looking, too."

"Don't be ridiculous," Kate snapped, angry at the telltale blush she felt rising on her cheeks. "I did not hire him because he's handsome."

"Oh! So he *is* handsome, then! Did you find Mr. Right, Kate?"

"Our Kate doesn't want to get married, remember?" Thomas said.

"Of course she does," Elizabeth insisted. "She just doesn't want to admit it yet."

"Let's not get started on that," Kate protested weakly. "I'm just following the apostle Paul's suggestion to stay single. Anything wrong with that?"

"I'll tell you what's wrong with that," Elizabeth responded, suddenly abandoning her jesting tone. "Being single requires a special call. Do you really believe you have that call?"

Kate felt the heat rising to her face yet again and swallowed in a vain attempt to dislodge the lump in her throat. She thrust out her chin rebelliously.

Elizabeth crossed her arms and raised one eyebrow. "Do you, Miss Logan?"

Kate slumped her shoulders in resignation. "No," she whispered.

"I didn't think so," Elizabeth replied. "Besides, you want to have kids, don't you?"

"Yeah. But not if it means I have to marry."

"That's usually how it's done," Elizabeth said with a chuckle. "Or at least it should be."

Thomas grinned too, and Kate pinned them both with a look. Being in business with two best friends from college had its drawbacks as well as its advantages. "Knock it off, you two. And who are you to preach to me, anyway? You aren't married."

"No, I'm not," her friend conceded. "But you can't fault me for not looking."

That was the truth, Kate thought, trying to hide a smile. Elizabeth was a striking woman, with long, blond hair that curled naturally. Her eyes were a luminous silver that attracted men like magnets. And she had a perfect smile, thanks to four years of braces.

"Well, there's no doubt you give it your best," Kate teased, winking.

Elizabeth was out every weekend, usually with someone new because she bored easily. Kate, on the other hand, hadn't been on a date in years. Which was, she reflected wryly, why she'd stopped mooning over something she was never likely to have.

Elizabeth gave a good-natured wave of her hand. "I just haven't found the right guy yet. But I will. And so will you, Kate Logan," she added firmly. "I've been praying that Mr. Right will soon be knocking on your door."

"Hope he brings a sledgehammer," Thomas muttered.

Both women simultaneously glared at Thomas's back and pulled a face at him, then hugged each other and burst into laughter, dissipating the unspoken tension in the room like sunshine cutting through fog.

Two

T odd, I'm so glad you're home!" A young woman with dark hair and eyes raced down the stairs of the town-house, taking the steps two at a time. "It came. It really came!"

"What came, Tam?" he asked, sweeping his sister into his arms for a bear hug.

"My acceptance letter. From the university."

He tried to steady his breathing, which had turned ragged at the announcement. A great part of him was rejoicing with his only sibling, knowing how hard she'd worked to get into med school. But anxiety overlaid joy, since he knew that the responsibility of getting her there rested squarely on his shoulders. He could almost hear the *ka-ching* of the cash register in the background.

"That's great, kiddo!" he said at last.

Tam scowled. "In case you haven't noticed, I'm not a kid anymore. I'm entering medical school this fall, and I've got a letter to prove it!" She waved the page beneath his nose for emphasis, then strutted around the room as if wearing high heels.

Todd laughed. Loudly clearing his throat, he snatched the page from her grasp and settled on the couch to read it. "Dear Ms. Jensen," he read, making his voice high and nasal. "We are happy to inform you...yada, yada, yada. Wow. I'm impressed."

She sat beside him and cupped his hand in hers. "You know what this means to me. I've always wanted to be a doctor."

"And so you will be," he assured her. It was his mother's

dying wish that Tam follow her dream, and it was the reason Todd was so desperate for an extra job.

Tam had worked her way through college, but med school was something else entirely. They both knew she'd be racking up thousands of dollars in student loans. He wanted to do everything he could to help her out.

"Well, talk about perfect timing. Guess what, Tam? I got a job today!"

His sister's dark eyebrows creased. "I thought you had a job."

"You didn't think Roseborough paid well enough to send you off to school now, did you?"

She frowned. "Send me off to school? Todd, I never expected—"

Todd ruffled her hair until she scowled and swung out of his reach. "Don't worry about it, kiddo. I told you I got a new job."

Tam looked suspicious. "Doing what?"

"Marrying people."

"Sounds fun. But way out of your league, big brother. What do you know about marriage?"

"Enough to write a doctoral thesis on the subject," he said, lunging for her. At the last possible moment, she stepped right, leaving him embracing empty air.

"See?" she prodded, as if proving a point. "Your only experience with romance is practicing on air."

"Which is all that's between your ears," he countered.

"Better than rocks."

They both laughed.

"I'll make it up to you," Tam vowed, throwing her arms around Todd's neck and burying her face in his chest.

"You already have, kiddo," he whispered into her hair. "You already have."

~ ~ ~ ~ ~

"Mom, I'm home!" Kate swept in the front door of the split-level house she'd called home all her life.

"In the kitchen, Kate!" her mother called from upstairs.

Her mother's voice sounded higher and more animated than usual, and Kate absently wondered what she had to be so excited about.

The answer was obvious the moment she stepped into the room.

Her mother was seated at the kitchen table with a woman Kate didn't know. It was clear they had been making plans of some sort, for the table was littered with business forms and brochures.

"Honey," Elise Logan said, rising to kiss Kate's cheek, "I'd like you to meet Marilyn Morgan, my real estate agent."

"Real estate agent?" She shook Marilyn's hand. "Um, nice to meet you." She felt she'd lost the gist of the conversation before she'd even walked in the door.

"Sit down, Kate," her mother commanded, gesturing to an empty chair.

"I'd rather stand," she countered more tersely than she intended. Under the circumstances, it was a wonder she could say anything at all. Her lungs felt as if they were in a vise.

Elise pinned her with a mother's glare, then continued. "I've been trying to find a good time to tell you this, but you've been so preoccupied lately trying to find a minister for your chapel."

Todd's handsome face flashed into Kate's mind but quickly dissipated as her mother's words took force. "Tell me what?"

In an unmistakable attempt to avoid meeting Kate's eyes, Elise fumbled with a colorful brochure. She looked to Marilyn for support, then blurted out, "I'm selling the house."

"You're *what?*" Kate screeched, coming to her feet. "Mom,

you can't sell this house. I was born here. Dad died here. You haven't thought this through."

Elise clenched her jaw, and her face took on its stubborn-as-a-bulldog look. "Sit down, Kate."

Kate sat.

"Marilyn," Mom continued, "I think we'll have to wrap it up for today. Kate and I need to talk. I'll call you Monday morning, okay?"

Marilyn nodded, stuffing papers into her briefcase with such abandon that it was clear she felt like an intruder.

Kate blushed, embarrassed at her momentary lack of manners. What had gotten into her? It must have been the shock of her mother's words. Shaking off thoughts of the inevitable confrontation awaiting her, she rose to her feet and smiled politely. "Marilyn, it was nice to meet you. Perhaps we'll see each other again sometime."

But not if I can help it, she thought, trying to keep her polite smile from turning into a grimace.

Marilyn patted Elise on the shoulder and excused herself.

Kate plunked back down in her seat and folded her hands on the table. No sense beating around the bush. It was just as well to get the unpleasantness over with. "Now what's all this about?"

Elise gave her a determined stare. "I've made my decision. I've spent the last three years moping about this house. I need friends, sunshine, laughter."

Kate interrupted. "But Mom, you can't take care of your—"

Her mother shook her head and held up her hands as if to ward off a blow. "I know what you're going to say. I've been over and over the arguments in my mind. It's time for both of us to make a break, Kate. You've been just as holed up here as I have, and you don't even have a disease to blame. It's my fault."

"But Mom," Kate said again.

"You need your own life. You need to get out and meet people. Meet a nice man. Get married, settle down. Give me some grandchildren."

Kate shook her head fiercely. "I don't want to meet a nice man and settle down."

"Well, you don't want to settle down with a not-nice one."

Kate didn't acknowledge her mother's joke.

Elise peered over the half-eyeglasses perched at the edge of her nose, looking for all the world like a wise old owl. "What are you going to do when your friends marry and start families of their own?"

"Thomas, married?" Kate hooted. "Now that I'd like to see. There isn't a woman on the planet who could put up with him for more than five minutes! Elizabeth, on the other hand..."

"It will happen," her mother insisted. "And when it does, you'll be all alone."

"What is really going on here, Mom? Why would you want to sell the house?" Kate attempted to steer the subject away from her pitiful excuse for a social life and back to the subject at hand.

Her mother sighed, suddenly looking weary and old. "I've been lonely since your father died. It's time for a change."

Kate's heart clinched. She knew the feeling well. Loneliness was so much a part of her life she rarely even noticed the quiet ache anymore. Unless someone specifically brought it to her attention, which was happening a little too often in recent days.

"Maybe so," she agreed, her voice hoarse. "But selling the house? Isn't that a bit drastic?"

"I don't think so. This house is way too big for the two of us. You have to admit that five bedrooms for two people is a bit excessive." She looked longingly around the country-style kitchen. "When Henry and I bought this house, we planned to fill it with children."

Kate reached across the table and squeezed her mother's hand. She knew how much her mother had wanted more children. But soon after having Kate, she'd discovered her multiple sclerosis. More childbearing was out of the question. Elise wasn't sure how long she'd be alive to care for the one child she had, or how difficult the degenerative disease attacking her body would make things.

But she had outlived her husband and was still going strong. Kate offered a silent prayer of thanksgiving for the time she'd had with her mother. She couldn't imagine a more courageous, faithful woman than Elise Logan.

"I've been praying about this," her mother continued, drawing Kate's thoughts back to the present. "I'm planning to move into a retirement community."

"A what?" she squeaked. "An old-folks' home? But Mom, you're only fifty!"

Elise laughed. "Not an old-folks' home, a retirement community. A neighborhood full of active seniors. I'll be able to make friends, learn to golf, have fun. And you won't have to provide for me. Besides the sale of the house, your father left me plenty to get by on."

"I didn't know you wanted to learn to golf." Kate swallowed hard, her mind reeling.

Her mother smiled gently. "There are many things you don't know about me."

"I guess." Kate felt a small knot of emptiness expanding into her chest. "But what about your MS? What if you have a bad day?" She didn't want to mention that Elise would continue to get worse until she eventually wouldn't be able to walk at all. "Who will take care of you?"

"They have a nursing staff on call. I'm not completely incapable, Kate."

Still struggling to come to terms with Elise's drastic words, Kate cringed at the resentment in her mother's voice. For so long she'd been her mother's only caregiver. Now, in one sweep of a hand, everything had changed.

It wasn't that she didn't believe Elise could do what she said she would do. A more cheerfully determined woman didn't exist. But to make such radical changes on such short notice was too much for Kate to comprehend.

"You're sure about this?"

Her mother nodded, excitement sparking from her eyes. "I'm absolutely certain this is the best thing for me."

"But what am *I* supposed to do?" Kate croaked through a dry throat. She sounded selfish and childish even to her own ears, but she couldn't help but blurt out the question that had been rising within her since walking into the house and finding a realtor present. It was as if her entire world had just flipped over.

"Oh, Kate, dear," her mother crooned, shaking her head. "You'll survive magnificently. You'll see." She reached out and squeezed her daughter's hand.

Kate noticed how much weaker her grip was than it used to be, but the spark in her eyes was as vivacious as always. She smiled weakly, knowing her own grip was none too sure at the moment.

"Get yourself an apartment," Elise continued. "Experience life on your own. I can't help but think that you'd be married by now if you weren't so busy caring for me."

"That has nothing to do with it," Kate denied vehemently. "I'm just not interested in getting married."

"Be that as it may, I'm selling this house. I'm going to call Marilyn in the morning and officially put it on the market."

"What about the memories?" Kate whispered, fighting tears and hating the weakness of spirit that put them there.

Elise stood and slowly limped to the back of Kate's chair. Placing her hands firmly on Kate's shoulders, she sighed. "It's hard for me, too, honey." She took a deep breath. "I know it's difficult for you to think about leaving, but you've got to trust me on this. It's the best thing for both of us. You wait and see."

Kate declined her mother's offer of a cup of hot tea, though her nerves could have benefited from the calming effect of the strong, sweet liquid. Instead she changed into a long flannel nightgown and rolled herself into bed a good two hours early.

So much so fast. Her emotions were swaying back and forth like a new aspen in a windstorm.

This house was *home*. To sell it was like selling her child-hood memories to the highest bidder. She curled into a ball, clasping her knees to her chest.

Memories swirled around in her head. Family dinners in the formal dining room on Sundays after church. Playing checkers with her mother next to the fireplace on a cold winter's evening. Slow dancing around the living room with her father, her small feet standing on Daddy's bigger ones as he taught her the steps.

"Daddy," she whispered into her pillow.

It had been seven years since his death, but she still missed her father's strong, quiet influence on her family. If he had lived, things might have been so different.

"Daddy," she whispered again, her voice cracking. "Oh, Daddy."

Soon her appeal to her father became a petition of prayer to her heavenly Father. Lifting her burden to the Lord, she quieted her soul and eventually drifted into a peaceful doze, her father's name still on her lips.

Monday morning found Todd anxiously awaiting his meeting with Kate. He'd planned to be early, but now every minute seemed an eternity. He squinted through the morning sunshine, watching for a car to appear on the main road.

Kate's face was easy to conjure in his mind. Her chestnut hair looked soft as silk. He wondered if it was as soft to the touch as it looked to be. And her eyes. A man could lose himself in those huge amber orbs.

He leaned against the hood of his truck and crossed his arms over his chest, inhaling a clean, deep breath of Rocky Mountain sunshine. *She's your employer*, he reminded himself firmly.

He stuffed his hands in his pockets and laughed quietly to himself. It must be the newness of the whole thing, his desperate need for a job, that made Kate so appealing. He would give it time.

And he could be her friend. He'd spent the evening praying about his job, and as usual, he allowed God to shift the focus of his prayers as he saw fit. But he'd been surprised to find himself praying for Kate.

He couldn't even begin to guess what she needed, but it didn't take a degree in theology or psychology to see that she wasn't completely happy. He hadn't had enough time with her to discover any more than her confession of faith, but for now, that was enough. God knew Kate Logan. And if Todd was meant to help her, God would help him find a way.

His thoughts were interrupted by the whirring of a Honda engine, and he thrust his meandering aside, preparing to greet his new boss.

Kate saw Todd the moment she pulled into the dirt road that served as the chapel drive. He was leaning casually against the hood of his blue Toyota 4x4, one foot braced against the bumper, arms crossed over his chest. He was more formally dressed this morning, with all-black clothing covered by a gray sport coat.

She laughed aloud. The man wore blue jeans and a denim shirt to a job interview, yet this morning, faced with hiking around a mountain retreat, he looked ready to lead a church service. Ah well. Cockeyed logic did not a bad pastor make.

She saw his eyes light up as she pulled into the drive, and he rushed to open the door for her. Grinning, he extended a hand to assist her out of the car.

Kate stared at his hand a moment, amazed at his casual chivalry. Men usually didn't rush to do anything for her. Hesitantly she placed her hand in his, mentally berating herself for the flush she felt rising to her cheeks. If she was going to blush every time she had to be in his presence, it was going to be difficult to get any work done.

His hand dwarfed hers, and she felt a shiver run the length of her body, as if she'd been exposed to a sudden draft. *This guy is tricky,* she thought, pulling herself to her feet and snatching her hand away from his grip. If she didn't watch herself, she might fall prey to his easy charm. The possibility alarmed her, and she stepped backward, further withdrawing from what she perceived to be a dangerous situation.

Unfortunately she stepped squarely on a jagged stone, which twisted her ankle and sent her sprawling. Were it not for Todd's strong arms scooping her up at the last possible moment, she would have had the dubious experience of landing in the dirt at his feet.

As it was, she landed securely in his muscular arms. It was difficult to decide which would be worse, but at the moment, she thought she might have preferred to eat dirt.

Another bolt of adrenaline shot through her, surpassing what she had felt when she lost her balance and knew she was going to fall. *See,* she thought grimly, grasping his arm in a natural reflex. She wanted to snatch her hand away again when she felt the curve of his biceps against her palm. *Even your subconscious recognizes danger when it sees it—him.*

"Careful, there," Todd said easily. "We can't have a pretty damsel in distress here. I left my white horse at home."

Pretty? Right. No man ever called Katie the Whale "pretty."

But the look on Todd's face was anything but teasing, and Kate's skin tingled under the intensity of his warm gaze. Was it her imagination, or did he hold her for a moment more than was necessary?

She struggled to regain her balance and gingerly tested weight on her throbbing ankle, hoping desperately for enough pain to keep her mind off her throbbing heart.

"Are you going to show me the chapel now?" he asked, his easy smile returning. He continued to hold his arms in midair, as if gauging whether or not she would be able to stand on her own two feet. "I tried the door, but it was locked."

Kate thrust a hand into her purse, digging for the keys to the door. "Pesky little things," she said, scowling. "Sometimes I think they swim around in here on their own."

"Perhaps if you carried less in your purse?" Todd suggested with a low chuckle.

"Adding insult to injury, are we?" Kate swung around and stomped to the door, refusing to acknowledge the bolt of pain that shot up her leg.

Tossing a glance behind her to see if he was following, she jammed the key into the lock, breathing deeply as the door swung open. The smooth, sweet combination of sawdust and pine assailed her senses, and the quiet peace immediately soothed her nerves, as it always did. It was part of what had attracted her to this tiny chapel in the first place.

That and the quaint A-frame shape and ornately carved pine pews. The entire front side of the building was a collage of stained glass, now luminescent in the rising sun. The building itself was made of thick pine trunks as supporting beams, with sawed pine board walls. The entire structure had been patched with tar and the roof roughly shingled. Even the door was made of pine, and the floor was covered with a light dusting of sawdust shavings.

It wasn't the scene of a royal wedding, but she knew instinctively that many couples looking for a small, intimate wedding would think it was perfect. It was exactly what she would look for...not that she'd ever be looking.

Todd came tramping in the doorway and stopped abruptly to gaze around. His eyes widened in awe as he considered the small chapel, and he whistled his surprise. "Wow! It doesn't look like much from the outside, but inside it's really something!"

She nodded. "It's lovely, isn't it?"

"I'll say. I've never seen anything quite like it." He scuffed through the sawdust, which clung to his black penny Loafers and buried itself in clumps on his socks. When he reached the pulpit, he turned and smiled.

"Kind of gives a new meaning to walking down the sawdust trail, doesn't it?"

Kate laughed aloud. It did rather resemble the sight of an old-time revival meeting.

"How are the acoustics?" he asked. "I notice you don't have a microphone."

She shrugged. "I have no idea. We haven't worked all the bugs out yet."

"No rush. Just curious."

"I'll put that on my list." Biting the corner of her lip, she began searching the contents of her purse for her Day-Timer.

"Hello!" Todd shouted.

It startled Kate so completely she nearly tossed the entire contents of her purse into the sawdust at her feet. "What are you doing?"

He gave a Cheshire cat grin, showing a full line of teeth. "Testing the acoustics for you."

Her eyes widened as he burst into song.

"Amazing Grace, how sweet the sound, that saved a wretch like me."

His rich baritone echoed through the chapel, sounding like a multitude rather than a single voice.

Angels, she thought as she absently seated herself on a pew. Her heart swelled in time to the music. *A multitude of angels.*

She closed her eyes as Todd continued, his deep, melodic voice meandering into the hidden places of her soul. The verse ended. Kate didn't want to open her eyes and break the moment, but she could feel his eyes upon her as surely as if he'd touched her. "Why'd you stop?" she asked quietly, looking up at him.

He walked down the aisle and extended his hands to her. "Sing with me?"

"What?"

"Sing with me. The acoustics in here are wonderful."

Kate snatched her hands away and turned her back on him so he wouldn't see the confusion she felt must surely be written on her face. Panic made the blood surge in her veins, and she struggled to keep her breathing slow and even.

"I...don't sing."

"You sing in church, don't you?"

"No," she whispered, lowering her eyes to the swirling sawdust patterns on the floor.

"No?" He sounded genuinely surprised. "They don't sing in your church?"

Kate laughed. "Of course they do. I just prefer to listen."

"Why? I'll bet you have a beautiful voice."

She forced herself to smile and meet his eyes. "I haven't tried to sing in a very long time. I...used to sing in a choir in junior high. "

"There you go, then," Todd said, smiling encouragement at her.

He was making a simple request. She was the one who was making an issue out of it. A scene from long ago flashed through her mind. A jumbled crowd of youngsters, pushing, shoving. Taunting. Laughing. Voices jeering.

Here comes the queen.

Look at that wad of blubber.

Queen Fat Girl.

Doesn't she know better?

Kate forced the memory back into the depths of her mind. She'd better cooperate before he started asking too many questions. "All right, all right," she said. "I'll sing."

Todd grinned and extended his hand and helped her to her feet. "Let's do it." He began the second verse of "Amazing Grace."

Kate cleared her throat and hesitantly added her voice to his.

He smiled and nodded, gesturing for her to continue. Sheer, transparent joy radiated from his liquid brown eyes, and Kate found herself drowning in their lucid depths.

We sound good together! she thought in amazement as her voice rose in confidence. She closed her eyes and lost herself in the music, so caught up in the beauty of the moment that she didn't even realize Todd was still holding her hand.

Todd knew. He couldn't have released her hand if his life depended on it, so completely was he swept up by her beautiful voice.

The voice of an angel.

He could see tears slipping from the corners of her still closed eyes. He heard his own voice turn gruff with an unnamed emotion and attempted a discreet cough to dislodge the pesky lump that had formed there.

She stopped singing, and her eyes fluttered open. She looked disoriented. And defenseless, like a deer caught in headlights.

Seemingly with a mind of its own, Todd's free hand reached out to caress her cheek, to wipe the unshed tears from her eyes.

Kate gulped and turned away from him, but not before he saw the look of sheer terror cross her face.

Dear Lord, what have I done?

He pulled his hands away as quickly as if he'd touched a hot stove. His fingertips still tingled from the feel of her skin, and his heart beat double time in his chest.

"Kate, I apologize. I didn't meant to upset you."

She spun around. "Apologize?" she demanded. "For singing with me?"

"I...I..." It was a rare moment that found Todd Jensen unsure of his words, but this was definitely one of them. He thought she was angry. Really angry.

Then suddenly she was laughing. Through her tears, she was *laughing*.

Three

T odd followed Kate back to town to Thomas's house, where Thomas and Elizabeth waited to meet their new employee. Again he was the epitome of a gentleman, hopping out the moment he'd parked the truck in the driveway in order to assist her from the car. He offered her a hand to steady her balance, then combed his fingers through his hair and smiled. "Ready, Kate?"

He looked so entirely relaxed that she had the curious impression that she, rather than Todd, was the one about to be thrust on display. She giggled nervously. "Are *you* ready to face the wolves?"

He chuckled. "Any friends of yours are friends of mine."

At her direction, they moved along the side of the ranch-level red brick house, which was lined with rows of multicolored tulips just beginning to flower in the spring sunshine.

A downward stairwell curved around the back of the house, and Todd clattered down the steps automatically, giving the door at the bottom a crisp knock.

Elizabeth opened the door, and Kate couldn't help but feel smug to see her friend's eyes widen at her first glimpse of Todd. What was surprising, however, was that Todd didn't seem to notice Elizabeth. At least not in the way Elizabeth was accustomed to being noticed.

His grin was friendly, but his attention quickly shifted back to Kate. He waved his arm and said, "Hurry up, slowpoke!" He held the door and gestured for her to enter ahead of him, his mouth quirked endearingly.

That smile is going to be my downfall, Kate thought in alarm, trying to quell her racing heart. She quickly looked away and moved to pass him. When she felt the light touch of his hand on her elbow, as if to guide her through a doorway she went through daily, she nearly jumped out of her skin.

His hand remained on her arm, and his featherlight touch flustered her even further, causing her to blunder through the requisite introductions. "Todd, I'd like to introduce you to my business associates and close friends, Thomas Quinn and Elizabeth Edwards." She gestured from one to the other. "And this is Father Todd Jensen, our new chapel minister."

"Glad to meet you, Father Todd," said Thomas, thrusting out his hand for a hearty shake.

"Welcome to the office, Father!" Elizabeth bubbled.

Kate was surprised that Todd didn't tell them to call him by his first name, as he had done with her. In fact, he seemed quite comfortable with their use of the word *Father.*

Elizabeth stepped out of Todd's vision, her eyes brimming with mirth, and made a marked survey of him from head to toe. Then she caught Kate's eye, quirked her lips, and nodded smugly. Her *I-told-you-so* was easy to read.

Kate shrugged and rolled her eyes. She didn't need Elizabeth to tell her Todd was handsome. She knew that he was that and more. The corner of her mouth twitched merrily as she considered how he would react were he to discover he'd just been sized up—and had passed with flying colors.

At least in the looks department. He would, she knew, have to pass muster in the character department as well, but she had no doubt he would charm both Elizabeth and Thomas as he had charmed her. Though she didn't trust any man, she admitted grudgingly—but only to herself—that she already felt comfortable with Todd.

Thomas laid a hand on Todd's shoulder. The two men were

a study in contrasts—Thomas tall and lithe with white-blond hair that curled around his collar, Todd with his short dark hair and broad build. What Todd lacked in height, he made up for in sheer muscle.

"Come over to my corner with me, Father," Thomas offered, "and I'll show you what I do."

Todd did his best to appear interested in Thomas's monologue on wedding photography, but he found his gaze crossing the room to where Kate was going over some accounting figures with Elizabeth.

Like the majority of women he met, Elizabeth appeared attracted to his calling. She wasn't afraid to show it, either—a little giggly, almost fawning. It made him uncomfortable.

Kate, on the other hand, wasn't at all like other women. She didn't hang on him or simper about his vocation. If anything, she held herself back, forcing him to draw her out. He couldn't charm her with the ease he was accustomed to, and that captivated him.

Judging from their experience in the chapel, he knew she felt things deeply, as he did, except she was afraid to let her feelings show. She was beautiful both in body and in spirit, but she was obviously unaware of her appeal.

She'd relaxed now and was laughing quietly with Elizabeth. The pain he had seen in her eyes diminished when she was with her friends, Todd saw, and he felt a sense of relief. Here, he surmised, she felt safe.

He wanted her to feel safe with him and vowed to make it so. Somehow he would win her trust. No doubt his competitive instinct was getting the best of him, for Kate would be a challenge to conquer, no doubt about that. The age-old thrill of pursuit coursed through him.

With a force of will, he turned his attention back to Thomas and his photographs, but try as he might, he couldn't keep his gaze from wandering time and time again in Kate's direction, capturing in his mind's eye her shining eyes and gentle smile.

Kate felt his eyes upon her even when she refused to acknowledge them, which she continued to do after the first time she'd met his gaze. He'd smiled and winked, making her breath stop in her throat.

Elizabeth continued to spout off figures with rapid accuracy. Kate knew it was a cover, knew her friend was purposely trying to draw attention their way. Todd's attention. Her stomach knotted at the thought. She didn't want Elizabeth to be attracted to Todd. Not in that way.

"Overall, business is booming," Elizabeth concluded rather loudly. "Even with the recent property purchase, we're making a tidy profit."

Kate felt rather than saw Todd approach. He didn't touch her, but she could feel him leaning over her shoulder. She dared a brief glance at his clean-shaven face, noting keen interest in his expression.

"Does that include the salary of your wonderful new chapel minister?" he asked lightly.

Elizabeth laughed. "Oh, don't you worry, Father. I didn't forget to count you in. I can already tell you're going to be an important part of this team."

Kate didn't miss the meaningful glance Elizabeth threw her direction, and a surge of relief flooded her heart. So Elizabeth wasn't interested in Todd after all—except as potential matrimonial material to foist on her.

The relief was promptly replaced by a surge of anger that warmed her cheeks. Why was everyone so all-out determined to marry her off? Didn't they have anything else to do with their time? It wasn't as though she couldn't take care of her own problems.

Not that Todd is a problem, she corrected herself. He wasn't—yet, though she acknowledged his potential to become a problem. A very big problem.

But only if she let him. And she wasn't about to let him. She scowled at Elizabeth, who only shook her head. Kate had the distinct impression she hadn't heard the last of her friend's opinions on the subject.

She stood and smiled up at Todd in a clear diversionary tactic. "You've seen what Thomas does. Would you like to have a VIP tour of the rest of the office?"

He smiled back at her. "If you're giving it, how could I refuse?"

Her smile wavered, and for a moment she could do no more than concentrate on restoring it. "Well, then, I hope you have good walking shoes on. As you can see, the place is huge."

He chuckled. "Can we start with the books?" he asked, gesturing to a wall of bookcases.

"We can, but I'm afraid you'll be disappointed. The only theology books we have are from our freshman Bible classes. Nothing you'd want to read."

"You might be surprised." He strode to the bookcases and ran a hand across the bindings of several books. He pulled out an exceptionally thick hardback volume and cradled it in his large palm as he flipped through the pages. "This one, I've got to admit, is way over my head."

He showed her the cover. *Corporate Accounting.*

Kate made a face. Numbers weren't *her* forte, either.

He lifted an eyebrow and glanced across the room to where

Elizabeth was sitting. "You really understand this stuff?" he asked, shaking his head.

"Every word," Elizabeth replied tartly. "And I'll bet you thought I was a dumb blonde."

"I didn't mean—" he started, but Elizabeth cut him off with a laugh.

"Relax. I'm joking. Though I really do use that material in my daily job here at Wedding Works."

He nodded, his eyes full of respect. "And these?" he asked, moving to another bookshelf.

"Those are my specialty," Kate explained. "Those on the top row are full of invitations from various printers. Our clients can browse through the books until they find what they're looking for."

"And these?" he asked, pointing to the next row.

"Cake decorations and catering. Flowers, real and silk. Two of the books are just accessories—bows, candles, and the like. On the bottom row I've got catalogs featuring various styles of tuxedos."

"I never realized planning a wedding was so complicated," Todd remarked, rubbing his head in a bemused fashion.

She burst out in a laugh. "You'd be surprised. I've tried to provide our clients with a full range of services, but even so, there are thousands of little details one can't overlook when planning the perfect wedding."

"You mentioned tuxedos but not dresses," he said as an afterthought.

"Right this way," she said, gesturing toward the open doorway of the consulting room.

His eyes widened as he entered and perused a wall full of photographs of bridal gowns. He leaned his closed fists on top of the solid oak conference table and gave a low whistle.

"Everything from quaint and old-fashioned to ultramodern," she said, proud of her selection.

"I guess," he said, following his comment with a shake of his head. He looked from the pictures to Kate and back, and she felt just the slightest tinge of confusion. She shook herself mentally and returned to the subject at hand.

"Think you can handle it?" she teased, as Todd absently continued to look around the room.

"I've got a lot to learn. They didn't teach us about this stuff at seminary."

"Well, don't sweat it too much. I take care of all the nitpicky stuff. You just have to marry them. And do counseling, of course. This is our consulting room, and we often use it with our clients. You're most welcome to use it for your counseling sessions."

He nodded and made a grunt of assent.

"Of course, feel free to meet wherever it's comfortable for you."

He grinned. "That'll be fine."

"Speaking of counseling sessions," she continued, "let me show you where your desk is. It's already loaded down with work for you."

He made an exaggerated groan as he followed her back into the office.

"Okay, so maybe I overstated the situation a bit. Most of the stuff on your desk is office supplies. I took the liberty of ordering what I thought you'd need to start, but just place an order from our office-supply catalog if you find there's something you need. We've got a standing account."

"Better and better."

"Somehow I don't think you'll overdo it on fluorescent pink sticky pads."

"Oh, you've found out my weakness," he teased.

She pointed to some papers on top of his desk. "There are three preliminary surveys from couples you'll need to contact for counseling. They're pretty thorough, and I hope you'll find you have a good basis established before your visits."

"Sounds like you've got everything covered."

Their eyes met, and Kate forgot to breathe. *Not everything,* she reminded herself. The armor around her heart felt painfully thin at the moment.

"Guess I'll get to work then," Todd said, and Kate was glad for the reprieve. For a while, at least, she'd be able to hide behind the cover of a silk-flower distributor's catalog. It wasn't much, but at the moment it was all she had.

A couple hours later, Kate looked up from her labor to find Todd standing over her shoulder, apparently watching her work.

"May I take you to lunch?" he asked, casually slinging his sportcoat over his shoulder.

Kate was about to agree when Elizabeth rushed up behind her.

"Oh, no, Kate, you can't leave yet. We haven't finished going over last month's figures!" Elizabeth slipped her arm through Kate's as if to draw her away.

"But I thought—" Kate began.

"No, you didn't have the chance to review the cash flow and balance sheet, remember?" Elizabeth broke in. *Don't be obtuse,* her eyes warned.

With an audible sigh, Kate gave into the inevitable confrontation, knowing full well there were no balance sheets to review. "Thank you for the offer, Todd, but as you can see, I'm still needed here."

Todd felt as if he'd been punched in the gut. He'd wanted the time alone with Kate, but it was obviously time she was unwilling to give. For one brief moment he'd thought she would accept his offer, thought he'd seen a glimmer of hope in her eyes. But then the shades had been drawn down, and she'd refused.

"Okay, then," he agreed, trying to erase the gruffness from his voice. "I may drop in again later, though. To show you the counseling program I've developed."

"Kate will be waiting for you to stop by," Elizabeth purred, shooting a triumphant glance at her friend.

Kate stuffed her hands in the pockets of her jeans skirt and glared at the floor, wishing most vehemently it would open up and swallow her. Or at least swallow Elizabeth before she could spout out something even more humiliating.

Elizabeth smiled and reached out a hand to Todd. "It was lovely meeting you, Father Todd. I just know we're all going to get along famously."

"I think so, too," he agreed, looking directly at Kate.

Kate didn't miss the way Elizabeth nudged her with her elbow at the words, and in an impish moment of response she elbowed Elizabeth back—hard.

To her satisfaction, Elizabeth grunted.

"What did you do that for?" Elizabeth demanded the moment Todd was out the door. She rubbed her rib cage and moaned. "That hurt."

"It was supposed to hurt. Do you think Todd won't pick up on all those innuendoes you're throwing his way? He's not stupid."

"No, but you might qualify," said Elizabeth, cocking her chin in the air. "I don't care if he does notice my hints. You certainly aren't making any moves."

"Making any moves!" Kate protested. "Of course I'm not making any moves." She held up her fingers and ticked off her reasons. "One. I've only known him for four days, during only two of which have I actually been in his presence. Two. I'm not the least bit interested in pursuing a relationship with Todd or with any other man, as you well know. Three. Even if I were interested in Todd—and I'm not saying that I am, mind you— but if I were, I'd be wasting my time. I don't have to tell you he's one of the best-looking men walking the planet."

"Um, excuse me," Thomas interrupted, coughing uneasily. "May I go now? You ladies will have to work this one out on your own. Just lock the door behind you when you leave."

"Did we ask you for your input?" Elizabeth demanded.

"Not like I'd give it to you even if you did ask, squirt," Thomas replied, tapping Elizabeth on the nose with his index finger.

Even more than being called squirt, Elizabeth hated to be tapped on the nose, as Thomas well knew. Kate could see an angry flush on her pale cheeks, and as Elizabeth wasn't one for holding her temper in check, Kate quickly took matters into her own hands.

"Thomas, darling," she said consolingly, "why don't you scuttle on upstairs before you get hurt?" She made a sweeping motion with her hands.

Thomas pulled himself up to his full height and thrust out his chest. "Men do not scuttle."

"Fine then," Kate agreed. "Stamp or stomp or whatever it is men do."

Elizabeth burst into laughter, and he scowled.

"Why don't you guys ever talk about me that way? The way you talk about Father Todd, I mean. Doesn't tall, blond, and handsome work for women anymore?"

Kate laughed and hugged Thomas around the waist. "Tall, blond, handsome, and nice. It's a great combination. We love

44

you just the way you are, Thomas. Don't you dare change a thing."

He looked vaguely consoled but continued to scowl.

"You're the best friend a girl could have, right, Lizzie?"

Elizabeth nodded grudgingly. "Even if you do butt into female business."

"No way," said Thomas, making for the stairs. "I'm most definitely butting out." He slammed the door behind him for emphasis, and the women burst into laughter again.

Elizabeth quickly sobered, crossing her arms over her chest in a manner Kate found more than a little intimidating. "All right now, enough sidestepping. I want details. All the details!"

"What details?" she asked innocently, though she knew very well to what her friend referred.

"What details, she says. What do I have to do, woman, smack you alongside the head with a baseball bat?"

"I'd rather you didn't."

"Please don't try to tell me there isn't something starting between you two."

"There isn't."

"I told you not to tell me that."

"Well, it's the truth." Kate set her chin stubbornly.

"You are not as blind as all that, Kate Logan."

"What do you mean?"

"There's chemistry brewing between you. Sparks flying, I tell you! Fireworks. Like the Fourth of July."

"Don't be ridiculous. Todd is gorgeous, not to mention the fact that he's a pastor. Give me a break."

Elizabeth grasped Kate rather roughly by the shoulders and forced her attention. "Give yourself a break. You can't tell me you didn't notice Father Todd looking at you. And he was, lots, even when you didn't notice. He's interested in you, Kate. Why is that so difficult for you to hear?"

Kate dropped her gaze.

"Look. Maybe you're not ready to pursue a relationship with him. But at least give him a chance to do the pursuing. Take it a step at a time and see where it goes. There's nothing to lose here."

Except my heart.

Kate shook her head vehemently. "He couldn't be interested in me. Look at me! My hair is mousy. And I'm fat. What could he possibly see in a woman like me?"

"Your lovely personality, perhaps? Your heart for God? Your sweet smile? Besides, your hair isn't mousy, it's a lovely chestnut color. And you're not fat. Haven't we gotten over that misconception yet?"

"You didn't know me in high school," Kate mumbled, afraid to look at her friend. Years of frustration balled in the pit of her stomach, roiling into a tidal wave.

"Well, you haven't looked in the mirror lately. You've grown up a lot since then."

Not inside, Kate thought. *Inside I'm still the fat, ugly fourteen-year-old everyone laughed at. And I can't bear to have it happen again.*

"No!" she cried, angrily swiping at the tears forming in the corners of her eyes. "He's not interested in me. What kind of friend are you, anyway? Raising my hopes so I can take a fall?"

She paused and choked on a breath. "I've worked hard to build a life for myself. I'm not going to ruin it by allowing a man to break my heart."

"Or make you deliriously happy. Did you ever think of that?"

"I'm not willing to take that chance. I'm smarter than that. I know a man like Todd wouldn't care for a woman like me."

Kate rushed to the door and swung it open wildly, her lungs heaving to force a strangled breath through her throat.

"I'm not going to dash my own head on the rocks. Not in this lifetime."

Four

A week passed, and things had finally settled down at Kate's office. Everything except her heart, that is.

Todd fit in as if he'd been along with the three friends through their college days. There was an easy rapport between them, the casual slinging of jokes, the serious moments in prayer every morning.

Maybe that was what scared her, Kate reflected, scribbling some specs for a satin gown in a steno notebook. The office was humming with quiet activity. Thomas was singing in a lilting tenor as he cleaned his camera equipment. From Elizabeth's desk came the quiet tink and whir of her adding machine.

Todd's desk was empty, which Kate tried not to notice. He kept his own hours, and for all she knew he wouldn't be in at all today. She scowled in annoyance at the way her heart fell at the thought.

"Wake up on the wrong side of the bed this morning?" came a familiar rich baritone from behind her.

She whirled in her seat. "Todd. What are you doing here?"

As soon as she said it, she realized how stupid it sounded.

"I work here, remember?" he said with a chuckle. "Unless I've been fired for showing up late?"

"I'm sorry. I don't know why I said that."

"No problem." He threw his black sports coat over the back of his chair.

"We do have a coatrack," she teased, trying to regain her equilibrium.

"Yes, but this way I can rush to the rescue in case someone has a stray cat up a tree somewhere."

"I see," she said dryly. "A regular hero, aren't you? And humble, too."

He grinned like the Cheshire cat.

"Did I hear the word 'hero'?" Elizabeth purred, sending a knowing glance toward Thomas.

A chill ran down Kate's spine as Thomas returned the look. Her two friends were up to something, and she had a sneaky suspicion it involved her.

"Speaking of heroes," Elizabeth said coyly, delivering Todd her best full-blown smile. "I don't suppose you play softball?"

If God sent a whirlwind to sweep her away, it wouldn't have been a fast enough escape for Kate. She had been arguing with her friends over the stupid church softball league for at least three weeks.

Unfortunately they were every bit as stubborn as she was and didn't have the good grace to give in, despite her continued and adamant refusal to cooperate with them. They simply refused to comprehend that there was no possible scenario in which she could be convinced to play softball. End of subject. At least she thought it had been.

"Well, do you?" Elizabeth leveled her eyes on Todd, arms akimbo.

He hadn't, Kate realized, given Elizabeth an answer. In fact, he looked rather at a loss for words, if his wide eyes and the way his jaw moved soundlessly up and down were any indication.

"I...er..." He raked his fingers through the short tips of his hair, making it stand on end. "Why?"

"We have this league at our church," Elizabeth began, but Todd cut her off.

"Oh, uh, well, I'm afraid I can honestly say I don't have time to play in a league this year."

"Todd, my man," Thomas said, stepping forward to clap Todd on the back in the universal brand of violence common to all men. "You've jumped the gun, here, buddy."

"I...er," Todd stammered. "Oh." He smiled widely and shrugged off his faux pas with a good-natured lift of his shoulder. "Wouldn't be the first time."

The least he could do is feel embarrassed, Kate thought, again thrown off balance by the ease in which Todd moved in his world. *I sure am.*

"Actually, what we had in mind is a lot simpler. Shouldn't take any time at all. And you're just the man for the job," Elizabeth purred.

"I...sorry, I'm confused. What job?"

"We're trying to get *Kate* to join the league," Thomas blurted before Elizabeth could respond.

Todd flashed her an amused glance before confronting her friends. "Then why don't you ask her?"

"We tried that already," said Elizabeth in a tone between pleading and exasperation. "She won't play."

"I see," he replied, his voice reminiscent of a father responding to bickering offspring. "Actually, I don't see. Where do I come into this?"

Elizabeth gave a melodramatic sigh. "We thought you might be able to give her a lesson or two—you know, a refresher course? She feels a little shaky in her skills."

What skills? The only shaking Kate wanted to do was to shake Elizabeth until her eyeballs rattled.

"Give her a...refresher course," he repeated.

"Well, of course, we'd do it ourselves, but with our present schedule we have all we can do to make it to the regular practices, never mind the games. And since you're not in the league..."

"I think—" Kate began, but Elizabeth cut her off.

"It wouldn't be too much bother, would it, Todd?"

Todd took a deep breath and let it out. "Of course not. I'd be glad to help."

Kate held her breath until her world began to spin.

Nice as well as handsome. Willing to go out of his way to help a fellow human being. Help her play softball, something she had no inclination to do and even less chance of being successful at.

Taking time out of his busy schedule to bolster a hopeless cause. How could Elizabeth have even thought to have mixed Kate up in this mess.

And however would she get out?

"Tam? Are you home?"

Todd stomped through the door and yelled at his sister. She flew down the stairs of the townhouse two steps at a time, her wet hair wrapped in a towel.

"What's eating you?" she asked, ruffling Todd's already bristling hair. "You look like something the cat dragged in."

"I *feel* like something the cat dragged in. What a day!" He swiped a hand down his face. The muscles knotting at the back of his neck gave warning of an impending headache. "I need your help with something."

"Sure thing."

"Don't you want to know what it is before you say yes?"

"Nope. I'll help."

He snagged her head in the crook of his arm and unrolled the towel from her hair with his other hand, knuckling the top of her skull gently with his closed fist. "You're going to get yourself in trouble one of these days, kiddo," he warned as she kicked and squealed. "I'll ask you to find me a wife or something—then what will you do?"

"Find you a wife, of course." Tam swept her leg behind his knees and sent him sprawling onto his back, then stood grinning over him, wet hair a dark, tousled mess.

"Where'd you learn to do that?" he groaned, theatrically shaking his head as if dazed by the fall.

"Self-Defense 101. One of the many benefits of a liberal arts education." She placed a foot firmly atop his chest. "You can't pick on me anymore, big brother."

"Pick on you? I never picked on you!"

Her sparking gaze dared him to deny the truth, and a smile twitched at his lips. "Well, no more than any respectable big brother."

"Now that I'm about to graduate from college, you have to start treating me like an adult."

"Mmmph," he agreed grudgingly. He saw an opening and grabbed for it. "Did your education happen to include baseball?"

It was a rhetorical question. Tam was a natural athlete, participating in every sport available—including four years of high school softball.

She looked down at him and placed her hands on her hips, her expression one of utter disbelief.

"Baseball? Why baseball?"

"Er...uh, softball, to be exact," he corrected mildly, coughing as her heel dug into his diaphragm.

She reached for his hands and pulled him to his feet, then grasped the front of his shirt in her fist and poked a warning finger into his chest. "Todd Andrew Jensen, stop talking in circles, and tell me what exactly you're talking about this instant!"

He brushed her hands away. "Hey! Easy on the shirt!"

"Todd…"

He shrugged and refused to meet her eyes. "No big deal. I just…promised a woman I'd teach her how to play softball."

"You promised a woman you'd teach her…Todd! You don't know how to play softball!"

He felt his face glowing and scowled. "Why do you think I'm asking for your help?"

"I can't…" she began, then her eyes lit with understanding. "Oh! Is she pretty?"

He clamped his jaw shut.

Tam nodded, looking thoroughly amused. "So. Todd Jensen is finally getting around to falling in love."

He managed to shake his head vehemently. "I'm not in love!"

"No?" Tam queried. "Well, I didn't say that, anyway. I said you're *falling* in love. Big difference."

"Like you would know. You're barely out of diapers, and you're an authority on love."

They faced off, two stubborn Jensens at an impasse.

Todd broke eye contact first. "So, are you going to help me out here, or not?"

"I'll help," she agreed. "On one condition."

"Yes?"

"You tell me her name."

He rolled his eyes. *Women! Even sisters! Especially sisters!*

But he needed Tam's expertise. He weighed the issue in his mind.

"Kate," he said at last, in a huff of breath.

Tam's smile brightened. "Kate. What a nice name." She socked Todd affectionately on the shoulder. "Let me run up and comb my hair, and we can go."

"Go?" He didn't like the sound of this.

She was already racing up the stairs. "My bat, ball, and mitt are in the linen closet—grab them for me? I'll see if I can't rustle up another mitt from my bedroom."

"But I thought we could just…"

She turned around, her dark eyes sparkling with laughter. "What, Todd? Sit down with a notebook and list the Twenty Rules for Good Softball?"

When he nodded, she snorted in amazement.

"You idiot bookworm! You can't learn to play softball by studying. You have to throw and bat and catch. And get grass stains on your knees!"

Or on his backside, which was probably where he would spend most of his time. Tam was a hard teacher, especially when it came to sports he had no real interest in learning. What had possessed him to agree to help Kate in the first place?

Tam reappeared and marched him out to the grassy area behind their condo, tapping a bat in her palm with just the slightest bit of menace. She eyed him from head to toe.

He stared back, refusing to be cowed by a stupid game. Bat, throw, catch. He'd played as a kid. Wasn't playing baseball like riding a bike, something you never forgot how to do? How hard could it be?

One thing he knew for sure—he would be gentle with Kate when *he* was the teacher. Grass stains indeed!

"I can't believe I let you talk me into doing this," Kate mumbled, slapping her freshly oiled, brand-spanking-new baseball mitt against her jeans-clad thigh. "I haven't played softball since high school P.E."

Butterflies danced the tango in her stomach. It was humiliating enough to be out in a park in broad daylight pretending to want to improve her skills in a sport she'd never once desired to play in her whole life, without having to be with God's handsomest creation while she did so.

Todd was dressed all in black—black jeans, black T-shirt, black sneakers, black baseball cap. The color brought out the depths of his dark eyes and heightened his ready smile.

She swallowed hard, forcing her gaze from the breadth of his chest. What had possessed her to agree to allowing his help? Running around chasing a ball was the furthest thing from controlled, adult, and respectable that she could imagine. Even further from romantic.

Oh, give it up, Kate, she snapped inwardly, irritated with her own thoughts. She might not want to be here, but she may as well make the best of it and see if she still knew how to play the dumb game. She would not let thoughts of Father Todd Jensen get in the way!

"So, where do we start?" she asked, trying for light and easy.

Todd's mouth curled into a frown as he glanced around at their varied equipment. He'd come supplied with a bat, an assortment of softballs, and a couple of well-worn mitts. He was obviously a master at the game, if his equipment was anything to go by.

Once she'd realized she was trapped into this enterprise, Kate had gone out and purchased a new softball, a mitt, and a genuine Rockies baseball shirt, complete with vertical stripes and three-quarter-length purple sleeves. She'd even thrown in a catcher's mask for luck. No one could accuse Kate Logan of doing things halfway.

But she was going to need a lot more than luck not to make a fool of herself. Only almighty God himself could save this day. Well, she'd give him a chance. She sure hoped he'd come through.

"Shall I hit a few?" she said, stooping to pick up a bat and testing it with a wide-arc swing.

"Good as anything, I suppose."

"You okay?" she asked, noticing for the first time how quiet he was. And he wasn't smiling.

"Hmm?" he asked, distracted. "Oh, yeah, sure. Right as rain. Just trying to figure out the best way to teach you to play."

He grinned, and Kate's heart skipped a beat. What that smile did to her mind should be outlawed! Maybe she was better off when he was distracted.

"Okay," he said, thoughtfully stroking the day's growth of beard on his chin. "I'll pitch, you hit."

Kate moved beside home plate and planted her cleated feet shoulder length apart. She recalled that much, anyway. What worried her were the fine points of the game.

Todd still stood next to the dugout, tossing a softball from hand to hand.

"Aren't you going to throw from the pitcher's mound?" she asked.

"Huh?" he asked, looking dazed. "Oh. Yeah. Of course."

He moved to the mound, then swung his arm back for the underhand pitch. "I'll try to…uh…I'll pitch you a slow ball, and you try to hit it, okay?"

"Is that all?"

Todd raised his eyebrows. "All?"

"I mean, don't you need to show me how it's done first? You just want me to swing at it?" She struggled with the urge to walk straight out of the ballpark and not look back.

"Well, yeah, sure," Todd answered, laughing. "Have you ever watched a baseball game on television?"

"Of course."

"Good, then. Just do it like the guys on TV."

"On TV. Sure. Okay."

On TV, any guy teaching a girl to bat would put his arms around her and cuddle her to his chest while he showed her how to swing! Somehow, she didn't expect Todd to be quite that helpful, though it couldn't hurt to hope.

Okay, so her very limited exposure to baseball had been the heroes of romantic comedies. Surely he didn't assume she watched the real thing?

She closed her eyes, and a picture of Todd wrapping his strong arms around her flashed through her mind. She could easily imagine his thick forearms and rippling biceps curling around her, could almost feel the peace his strength would lend her.

But she would *not* think about the emotions he stirred in her. Not today. Not ever.

"Take a few practice swings," he suggested.

She swung the bat several times. It was heavy and drooped in the follow-through. But what could she do? Bats didn't come in men's and ladies' sizes, did they?

"Choke up on the bat."

"Choke on it?"

A low rumble of laughter came from his chest. "Not choke *on* the bat. Choke *up*. Move your grip higher."

"Oh." She choked up.

Todd whooped and threw the ball.

Kate watched it coming at her as if in slow motion. Pulling the bat back to shoulder level, she tried to swallow, but her throat was as coarse as the sand under her feet. The butterflies in her stomach had grown tired of the tango and had switched to the cha-cha.

Left, right, cha-cha-cha.

Left, right, cha-cha-WHACK!

She swung, hitting the softball with a resounding crack of the bat.

Todd's jaw dropped as his gaze followed the ball. It went well over his head, dropped to the ground behind him, and rolled into the playground.

"Yes!" she screamed, dropping the bat and throwing her fists up in the air in the symbol of victory. "And it's out of the ballpark, folks! Kate Logan hits the home run that saves the day! And the crowd goes wild!"

She whistled and hollered on behalf of the imaginary crowd as she jogged up to the pitcher's mound, where Todd still stood staring at the ball, which had landed smack dab in the middle of the playground.

"Well?"

His silence unnerved her. Her heart pumped a mile a minute. She'd done it, she'd really done it! What's more, she'd done it well!

"That was…spectacular!" he said at last, his voice low and gruff. He cleared his throat and swiped a hand across his jaw. "How'd you do that?"

"It's a company secret." *Thank you, dancing butterflies.*

He made a sound in the back of his throat that was a cross between a grunt and a groan. "I think maybe we should try catching."

"Catching? I can do catching. I even have a mask." Her confidence had grown leaps and bounds with that one resounding *crack*. And maybe a little by Todd's encouragement.

She rushed over to the neat pile of equipment and selected her mask, then ran back behind home plate and crouched low. "Hey, batter, batter, batter…swing!"

He chuckled and shook his head. "You don't need a mask to catch unless you're the catcher. And you don't have to squat on your haunches, either."

"Oh." The wind taken from her sails, she stood and pulled the mask off, knowing she was exposing her flushing face. She tossed the mask onto the ground near her feet, refusing to meet his eyes, quickly reverting to the old Kate. The loser Kate. "What do I need to do, then?"

She hazarded a quick glance at his face. He looked grim, and she scowled. It was just a slight misjudgment, after all. What, he expected her to know everything on her first try? She wasn't going to be a softball star, probably not even a decent player. There weren't many things in this world she *was* really good at, especially in the athletic realm.

She cringed inwardly, remembering the humiliation of being kicked off the elementary school tumbling team. Though it was many years ago now, the words stung her heart as if they were uttered yesterday.

I'm afraid she's going to get hurt, Mrs. Logan. It would be best for her to withdraw from the team.

What her instructor had really meant was *She's no good, and I don't want to embarrass the rest of the girls.*

Even a second-grader could figure that out.

"Kate?" Todd's voice pierced through her haze, the rich timbre of his voice touching her every bit as tangibly as the hand brushing her shoulder.

Dashed from her daydream, she stared up into liquid brown eyes, full of concern.

"I lost you there for a minute," he said, smiling gently and chucking her under the chin. "Is everything okay?"

The mere size of him, standing so close to her, was enough to put her nightmare to rest. She found such comfort in his gaze. A woman could lose herself in eyes like his.

"I'm sorry," she mumbled.

"No prob, Bob," he replied promptly. "I mean, Kate."

She laughed and fanned her hands at him, brushing his comment aside. It was only then that she noticed the two boys, she guessed their ages to be about ten, standing at her side, looking up at her with a smudge-faced mixture of annoyance and boredom.

They were dirty, scrawny, and toting baseball bats.

"Are we gonna play, Father?" one of them asked.

At Kate's inquiring look, he explained. "While you were daydreaming, I shanghaied these two fellas to pop you some balls."

"Oh—uh, that's nice of them." She turned to the boys. "Thanks, guys," she said, but her insides knotted from the effort. She really didn't want to look stupid in front of a couple of preteen boys. Looking foolish with Todd was more than enough for one day.

Which brought another question to mind. "What about you?" she asked, pulling her mitt onto her left hand. "Are you going to field with me?"

"Me?" He mumbled something unintelligible under his breath. "Not a chance. I'm coming out to give you pointers."

"I see." Obviously he didn't want to embarrass her by showing off his own skills. What a sweet guy.

She punched her right hand into her mitt as she'd seen other baseball players do. "Well, I'm as ready as I'll ever be."

He smiled encouragement at her. "I'm sure you'll do fine."

"How could I not, with a teacher like you?"

To her surprise and relief, Todd blushed to the tips of his hair. So, he wasn't perfect after all!

Five

K ate surprised even herself.

She was respectable at softball! If Todd's enthusiasm was remotely accurate, she was even good at it. At least she was off to a decent start. In a single afternoon, she was batting, pitching, and catching with surprising sufficiency.

From her seat in the passenger side of Todd's pickup, she flicked a surreptitious glance in his direction. It was thoughtful of him to offer her a ride home, since she'd walked to the park loaded down with her gear.

But then again, it seemed everything Father Todd Jensen did was thoughtful and generous. She couldn't imagine a better man for a pastor, or for a—Well, that didn't matter. She was ready to face the church softball league, or at least as ready as she'd ever be. She couldn't help but wonder if her prime performance had anything to do with her coach.

He was patient and soft spoken, unlike some of the members of her church who played on the team. It wouldn't be easy exposing herself to them, giving others the opportunity to ridicule her.

But Todd would be there. He'd promised to attend the first practice, to give her moral support and whatever pointers he could offer. A regular knight in shining armor. And of course, Thomas and Elizabeth would be there, since they were the ones who'd pushed her into this in the first place.

Todd pulled the truck into her driveway. She took a deep breath and sighed. He hadn't spoken during the short drive home, but it wasn't an awkward silence. It wasn't often she could share a companionable silence with someone. She usually worried about what the other person was thinking.

But Todd wouldn't be thinking *anything* about her, certainly not anything bad, and that knowledge gave her peace. Moments of such serenity were few and far between, and she wasn't ready to relinquish this one.

"Would you like some iced tea?"

Todd tipped his baseball cap back on his forehead and smiled. "Sounds terrific. I'm parched." He shut down the engine and gestured that he'd get the door for her.

She waited. It was easy to get used to being pampered.

He held his hand out to help her, and she willingly grabbed it, enjoying the skitter of electricity that bolted up her arm at his touch. She could certainly climb down from the cab without assistance…but why would she want to do that? The smile in her heart reached clear to her toes.

The house was quiet when they entered. "This way to the kitchen," Kate whispered over her shoulder.

"Okay," he whispered back. His breath was warm on her ear. "Why are we whispering?"

"I live with my mom," she answered, feeling her cheeks warm under his scrutiny. "She's probably napping."

When he didn't respond, she continued. "She's getting up in years." Fifty wasn't exactly over the hill, but better to say that than to tell the whole truth. "She needs someone to take care of her. She has a…"

She paused, wondering how much she should say. Elise Logan was a proud woman, and Kate was certain her mother wouldn't want her blurting out scads of personal information to a complete stranger.

"…condition," she finished weakly.

"I'm sorry to hear that," was his genuine response, the very picture of a pastor's concern. "I'll add her to my prayer list."

"Thank you. I'm sure she'd appreciate that." She experienced a flash of irritation for feeling the need to rationalize her lifestyle to Todd. Mom needed her; that was all there was to it. And it was nobody's business but her own why she still lived at home.

As she entered the kitchen, she glanced over her shoulder to see his reaction to her statement, and nearly tripped over her mother, sitting cross-legged on the floor, rolling a knickknack in newspapers.

She supposed she should have noticed that the kitchen light was on, but she'd been so wrapped up in her thoughts of Todd that it hadn't registered.

Her gaze was immediately drawn to the object of her mother's efforts: two large U-Haul boxes already half loaded with newspaper-covered items. Half full and counting.

Kate's chest tightened like a vise, forcing the breath from her lungs. "What are you doing?" she asked.

For a long moment her mother's expression was one of reserved defiance, but then she looked over Kate's shoulder. Her cheeks took on a rosy glow and her eyes a dangerous sparkle as Todd moved into the room.

Kate gave her a warning look, but Elise chose to ignore it. This was the first time Kate had ever brought a man to the house, and she had the sinking suspicion her mother was going to overreact. And there wasn't a thing Kate could do to stop her.

Rising to her feet, Elise wiped the newsprint from her hands with a wet rag, then held out a hand to Todd. "I'm Elise Logan, Kate's mother." She lifted an inquiring eyebrow, clearly taking his measure.

Todd smiled and pumped Mrs. Logan's hand. She had a firm grip and was not one iota the invalid he'd pictured in his mind at Kate's description. He was expecting an eighty-year-old in a wheelchair, not the vivacious fifty-something staring back at him in open challenge. Other than a minor limp when she walked, Elise Logan appeared the picture of health.

He realized he'd unintentionally stepped into daughter territory, with a mom on the prowl. He was being sized up like a potential main course, and he experienced a moment's unease. He really didn't care to be the prize cut in a meat market. But he thought he could see a flicker of amusement in her gaze, so he brushed off his first impression.

Elise probably treated all the men Kate brought home as potential sons-in-law. What decent, self-respecting mother wouldn't? She couldn't know that he wasn't in the market for a relationship, that his concern for Kate was purely friendly. And pastoral.

Liar.

He pushed the thought away, chuckling inwardly, then relaxed his posture and broadened his grin. "Don't worry, I haven't asked her to marry me yet. I wanted to meet you first."

Relying on humor had always worked for him, but this time he wished he'd stuffed a sock into his mouth instead.

Elise burst into choked laughter, but Kate blanched and began to sway.

He quickly moved to her side and put a hand on her elbow, just to be on the safe side. Maybe she'd had too much sun.

"Sit down, Kate. You look a little pale." He led her to a kitchen chair and gently seated her.

Her gaze cut into him, a startling mixture of disbelief and something else, something he couldn't quite put his finger on.

He shrugged an unspoken apology for his words.

It was just a joke, meant to put everyone at ease. Maybe his choice of topics wasn't exactly divinely inspired, under the circumstances, but at least he'd tried.

"Pardon the mess." Elise made a sweeping gesture. "I'm sure Kate told you we're in the process of moving."

Moving? Kate was moving? When had this transpired? She hadn't said anything about leaving, and he couldn't imagine working day in and day out with Thomas and Elizabeth alone, however nice they might be. He'd miss Kate's velvet laugh, something he hadn't heard enough of yet to drink his fill. He wondered about the tugging sensation that filled his chest. Then another thought struck him like a punch in the gut.

What if he didn't have a job at all?

He questioned Kate with a look, willing his expression devoid of emotion. There was no sense jumping to conclusions when Kate could no doubt clear his mind with a word. Maybe it was a local move.

And her mother certainly appeared eager.

Kate shook her head violently but didn't clue him in on the situation.

He looked to Elise for help.

She moved to Kate's side, efficiently distributing knick-knacks, collector edition plates, an assortment of kitchen utensils, and handfuls of newspapers. "You two may as well make yourselves useful while we talk."

Kate smacked the newspapers down sharply on the table, making him wince inwardly. "I offered him iced tea, Mother, not a job."

"Well, actually, she did that, too," Todd cut in, sensing a storm brewing. "I'm the new pastor for Wedding Works. Father Todd Jensen," he added.

"Father?" Elise repeated, her eyes widening. "Well, this *is* a surprise. Kate, you didn't tell me—"

"I didn't have the chance," she snapped, then yanked the refrigerator door open with such force the handle banged against the counter.

If he didn't know better, he would have said she was pouting. Her bottom lip *was* jutting out just the tiniest bit. With her sweet, round face, she looked as adorable as any toddler, yet every inch a woman. He couldn't help the reaction that swept through him, the protective instinct that spurred him to make her smile again.

Her gaze met his, and it was as if he were looking into the mirror of her soul. Again he glimpsed pain in those amber depths. And again he vowed to be her friend.

"Did you know," he said, turning to Elise, "that we have a famous softball player in our midst? Move over, Babe Ruth."

"Softball? My Kate? I didn't know she was interested in the sport!" Elise sounded genuinely surprised. And pleased.

"I'm not," Kate remarked dryly, crossing her arms over her chest and glaring at Todd. "Not Babe Ruth and definitely not interested."

"Then why…?" Her mother let the sentence drop.

"In a word, badgered, bullied, and abused."

"That's three words," Elise commented.

Todd could see where Kate got her sense of humor; only her mother seemed more relaxed and inclined to use what she'd been given. He held up his hands in protest as Elise pinned him with her gaze. He could tell she was teasing by the gleam in her eye.

"Not me!" he said aloud. "I'm just as much a victim as Kate here."

"Suckered into helping the hopeless." Kate sighed loudly

and shook her head in mock distress. "Poor man."

He narrowed his gaze on her. It wasn't the first time she'd put herself down since he'd known her. What would cause such a lovely woman to do that to herself?

Father, help me reach her with your love.

"Do I sense Elizabeth's hand in this?" Elise asked keenly, eyeing Todd with new interest.

Kate just hmmphed.

"Don't let her fool you. She can bat, pitch, and catch with the best of them."

"With you, anyway," Kate amended. "The rest is left to be seen."

"Stop selling yourself short," he said, hoping his fervent words would make a crack in her armor. "If you don't believe your own eyes, believe me. You're a natural."

Their eyes locked. He willed as much strength into his gaze as he could muster, knowing this was an important turning point in earning her trust. That he wouldn't know Babe Ruth from Adam was irrelevant. She *was* a good player—had a lot more natural ability than *he* did. He let her read the truth in his gaze.

After an agonizing pause, she shrugged her shoulders and broke eye contact. "Well, just don't forget I told you so when I make a fool of myself at practice."

"I wouldn't miss it for the world," he countered. "I'll be easy to recognize since I'll be the one gloating."

"Iced tea, anyone?" Elise interrupted brightly, her interlude a symphony of impeccable timing and grace. Drinks had been forgotten in the turmoil of conversation, and now she served them frosted glasses from a tray as if she'd expected company all along.

Todd took a long pull from his glass, and Elise nodded smugly and put down her tray.

"I expect repayment for that, you know," she said, gesturing to the newspaper-ridden floor. "In the form of help. 'Whatever your hand finds to do, do it with your might,' you know."

Todd laughed. "'For God will bring every work into judgment,'" he countered easily.

Mumbling under her breath, Kate shuffled the strewn newspapers into a pile of sorts, then went to the cupboard and banged the door open, removing an old set of Corelle dishes they no longer used.

"Do I get any of this stuff, or does my experience of being dumped into the real world include sleeping on the floor and starving to death?"

Elise scooped up a newspaper and crumpled it, then beaned her daughter in the head with her handmade missile. "Of course, you nitwit."

"You're not moving?" he asked Kate, unable to stem the tide of relief that flooded through him. "Just your mom?"

"Oh, no, we're both moving," she informed him in a controlled monotone. He could see the telltale muscle working at the back of her jaw. "Different places. Mom's decided it's time for her to exchange her active lifestyle for an old-folks' home." It was an exaggeration on both counts.

"Retirement community," Elise corrected absently. Her voice sounded tired, as if she'd made the same revision a thousand times.

"Really?" he asked, his interest piqued. "Which one?"

"Roseborough. I've been searching for quite some time, and it's exactly what I've been looking for."

Kate's head bobbed up to flash a surprised look at her mother, but it quickly disappeared.

Todd finished wrapping a plate and nodded vigorously. "You'll love it!" he enthused. "I personally think it's the best community in the entire Western world! Golf, tennis, swimming. Not to mention a wonderful team of nurses on call twenty-four hours a day. You name it, they've got it! You couldn't ask for more!"

"And just how, precisely, would you know?" Kate asked.

He opened his mouth to answer, but with one look at Kate, he clamped his mouth shut again. Now was not, he decided, the appropriate time to mention that his other job was at Roseborough. It had been on his résumé, but she'd apparently forgotten.

"I, er…I've visited there," he finished lamely. "It's nice, Kate. Really."

She turned away from him, a guttural sound of disbelief escaping from her throat.

Elise sighed and patted Todd on the arm. "A tough sale, that one," she said, her voice low and confidential. "We'll both have to work on her."

It just wasn't fair. Kate had lived with her mother for most of her life, yet Todd managed to worm his way between them with little more than his winsome smile.

And as for Todd—well! She certainly hadn't hired him to butt his nose into her personal affairs, never mind side with her mother in an argument she was already clearly losing.

And it didn't help one bit for her mother to get up right in the middle of the afternoon, pleading a bad MS day and the desperate need for a nap and hinting broadly that the two of them should continue working on their own.

Whether she was really in pain or playing errant match-maker was questionable. Either way, it painted a clear, focused picture of Kate's dilemma. And it furthered her desire to dig a deeper hole in which to bury herself.

She rolled newspaper around a glass and set it grudgingly in her box. Her U-Haul box.

So it had finally come to this. She'd always known she would end up alone, had been mentally preparing herself for the time. So why did it hurt so much? It wasn't that she was afraid of living alone. She had a full life and close friends. Life centered around her work, but that suited her just fine. She wasn't complaining.

What she didn't want to be was lonely. And sitting here in a warm, cozy kitchen with Todd just accentuated her fears, gave her a sharp reminder of what she'd be missing. It was too domestic a scene not to consider the obvious, remember that she never would have someone to work with, play with, cry with. Share her life with.

Someone to care.

She was being rejected as her mother's caretaker, and she didn't need her mother to put the thought into words for it to be true.

Somehow, someway, she had failed. She'd done her best, but her best wasn't enough where Mom was concerned. The nip of rejection stung deep in the ache of her chest.

But never mind her—she was more than a little hesitant about her mother's living alone, Todd's enthusiastic recommendation aside. No one loved Elise as Kate did, and she'd put that up against a good deal of the medical knowledge an impartial nurse just putting in her hours would bring.

She couldn't help it if she worried. Her mother could still walk, albeit with a limp, but she was often in pain, especially at night. She might joke about feeling like a kid again, but her MS was very real.

What if there was no one to help her when she needed it?

"So what gives?" Todd asked quietly.

Kate snapped her head up so quickly she bit her tongue.

None of your business was her initial reaction, but when she met his gaze, she found there only simple interest and—compassion. Her defenses could weather an argument, but his gentle response was her undoing. How could she pick a fight with a man who clearly *cared* for her?

Yes, it was purely pastoral, because he was such a genuinely good, kind man, but for now, it was enough to get under her skin. A plethora of emotions roiled in her stomach, then washed through her body in waves. Fear. Distrust. Wonder.

And joy!

She closed her eyes, pushing the darker emotions away even as she embraced this newfound freedom.

She could talk to Todd, and he wouldn't judge. Listen, yes, and care. But not condemn.

She opened her eyes, allowing his smile to distract her for the tiniest moment. Then she licked her lips and plunged in. "I know it's unusual for a twenty-six-year-old to be living with her mother," she began.

"Don't apologize, Kate," he cut in, continuing to wrap sundry kitchen items as he spoke. "It's obvious you love your mother. Your compassion does you credit. Not many young women would put their family before everything the way you have."

She blushed fiercely and ducked her head to hide her flaming cheeks.

He waved a plastic spaghetti fork under her nose. "Which one of you gets this?"

"Me, definitely. My cooking skills are limited to boxed casseroles and opening a jar of Prego spaghetti sauce. Mom can't get around all that well, but she always…" Her sentence drifted off as her throat tightened around the words.

He dropped the utensil into the box marked for Kate and cleared his throat. "You like Italian?"

"Food, dressing, or actors?" she quipped, trying desperately to lighten the mood.

He chuckled and shook his head. "Sylvester Stallone I am not."

No way, she thought. *You're much better.* She'd take Todd over Sly any day of the week.

"I do, however," he continued, "make a mean lasagna. When you're set up at your new place, you'll have to invite me over and let me cook you dinner."

"Gladly," she said dryly, "if you don't mind cooking in a homeless shelter."

He chuckled, then his face sobered, making Kate's stomach flip like a pancake. "Do I hear a little self-pity?" he asked gently, his gaze prying more than his words did.

Taking a mental step backward, she opened her mouth to deny the accusation, then closed it again.

He was right. She was feeling sorry for herself. She should be trusting God to work out the details instead of refusing to admit she had a problem.

Tentatively she explored these new thoughts. She'd been in denial for so long, she'd neglected to look at the positive side of her circumstances.

A place of her own. A place she could decorate any way she chose. No more tiptoeing through the house in the middle of the afternoon, afraid she might wake her mother from her nap.

And Todd had promised to visit.

Her heart warmed at the thought. "Thank you," she whispered, unable to articulate her feelings.

"Thank you?" he echoed, his eyes widening. "I thought you

were going to bite my head off." He raked his fingers through his hair, spiking the ends in every direction. "Which I deserve for that brainless comment," he added in an undertone. "And I call myself a pastor."

She reached for another plate. Anything to keep her hands busy. A pastor he might be, but he was also a man. A very attractive man, even with the ends of his hair all ruffled.

Especially with the ends of his hair all ruffled. It was all she could do not to smooth down his rumpled locks, to see for herself if that scrumptious dark hair was as soft to the touch as it looked.

She hazarded a glance at him from beneath her lashes. He was smiling at her, his head crooked to one side as he tried to make eye contact with her beneath the shield of her bangs.

He looked like a bedraggled porcupine, and she could no more resist the impulse to touch him than to stop her heart from hammering every time he smiled. She reached out her hand, choppy and hesitant, until she felt the uneven thatch of his hair under her palm. It was soft, and surprisingly thick for as short as he wore it. She smoothed it back, her hand quivering.

He didn't stop her, though she could feel the crackle of electricity intensify between them. She watched, mesmerized, as the muscles near his throat contracted and he swallowed.

"My sister says I look like a terrier when I fiddle with my hair that way," he said, his voice rich and deep. "Bad habit."

She snatched her hand away. "Not so bad," she corrected mildly, cradling one hand in the other. "Not nearly as horrendous as self-pity."

Color rose to his face, even through his unusually healthy tan, considering it was still early spring.

"Me and my big mouth," he grumbled. "My mother used to

wash my mouth out with soap when I said something unkind. But did I learn from that? N-o-o-o! Of course not!"

"Do I hear a little self-pity?" she asked quietly, smothering a smile. When his eyes widened, she broke into a grin. "Back-atcha!"

"In spades," he agreed. "Shall we have a pity party together? We make a fine team."

Her breath caught in her throat. *A fine team.* "If we don't team up and get this mess cleaned up, I'm going to be here till midnight," she said, wondering if he was aware her voice was squeaking.

"This?" He gestured to the newspaper-strewn kitchen. "Between the two of us it'll take us five minutes. Then we can order in pizza for the three of us, my treat."

"Five minutes?" she asked doubtfully, but her heart was buzzing with contentment.

"Hey, I said we made a fine team, didn't I?"

Six

"Condo, townhouse, or apartment? Or did you want to buy a house?" Todd plucked a renter's guide from the grocery-store display and began thumbing through it.

Kate sighed audibly. "I don't know. A house seems a bit much for one person. What do you think?"

Again, he'd gone well beyond the call of duty in offering to help her look for someplace to live. He was certainly willing to go the extra mile for her. What she couldn't figure out was *why*.

Todd stroked his chin thoughtfully, his fingers lightly brushing over a day's growth of beard. He knew he should have shaved since he was spending the day with Kate, but Saturday was his day off. The rest of the week he pleased others; on Saturdays he pleased himself, up to and including rising late, dressing like a slob, and being a couch potato all day. But he should have shaved for Kate.

"Well?" she queried impatiently.

"I think I should have shaved."

"Todd! Hello! Planet Earth, here. I was asking about a house?"

"Oh. Yeah." He could feel his face warm under her scrutiny and was suddenly thankful for the whiskers covering his cheeks. "Rent, then?"

"Rent," she echoed, selecting a variety of rental guides from the display. "Okay, we'll start there. I think I've got one of everything. Let's go." She grabbed his arm to steer him out the door.

It occurred to him that it was the first time she'd touched him of her own volition. He looked down at her soft, small hand resting on his forearm. She was so small next to him, giving her an air of vulnerability that was exaggerated by her present set of circumstances. He put his hand over hers.

She looked up into his face and smiled. "I'm going to live through this, you know," she said quietly. "Even if I am presently acting like an oversized infant. 'For when I am weak, then I am strong.'"

"Kate, you're not..." His voice sounded strangled even to him. The desire to take her in his arms and cuddle her tight to his chest was nearly more than he could handle.

He dropped his hand from hers and stepped a safe distance away. Well, maybe not *safe*. He couldn't very well move to China to elude her warm, amber gaze and the soft smile that lit up his heart. More to the point, he didn't want to escape.

He unlocked the passenger side of his truck and extended a hand to help her in. Any discomfort he was feeling was his own problem, he decided. He'd just have to get control over it. He couldn't rev up like a motorcycle every time he had to touch her or he'd be in big trouble, since they had to work together on a daily basis.

"Let's look at townhouses," she decided, pulling one magazine from the pile on her lap. "I've decided I do want to rent. My life is pretty unsettled right now. Who knows where the next year will take me?"

Todd's gaze snapped to hers, but she looked back at him with wide, guileless eyes. He forced his shoulders to relax. Who knew, indeed?

Blowing out his breath in a huff, he made an abrupt U-turn on the highway.

Kate screeched, grabbing for the dashboard to keep from bumping her head on the ceiling of the truck. "I would like to live long enough to *find* a place to live, thank you very much."

He pressed his lips together to keep from smiling. Or frowning. He wasn't sure which.

"Where are we going?" she demanded.

"I know of a place for rent. Nice neighborhood. Close to a grocery store. Thought you might like to see it first. As somewhere to start."

Her eyes clouded, but she nodded her assent.

Todd tightened his grip on the wheel. "I sense this is really a hard time for you," he said gently. "I don't mean to pry or preach, but are you letting the Lord walk through it with you?"

She flashed him a startled glance, then grimaced. "That may be the one part of my life that's stable right now. I'm clinging to God. At least he never changes."

He could hear the apprehension in her voice and thought he was beginning to understand what was troubling her. "How long have you known about your mother wanting to sell your house?"

"She sprang it on me a few weeks ago. I had no idea she wanted to move."

"That has to be hard for you."

"You don't know the half of it. I grew up in that house. My father—" she choked up and fished in her purse for a tissue—"my father died there." She looked up at him then, pleading for him to understand.

He reached across the cab and took her hand, squeezing it lightly. "My parents died in a car crash two years ago."

"I'm sorry," she said quietly, and Todd felt a familiar wave of grief rush over him.

He allowed the pain to run through him without hindering its course, knowing it was better to embrace grief than ignore it. It was less intense than at first, when the shock of death had sent his faith reeling, but once in a while, like now, grief crept up on him again.

"We sold the house last year." His voice was gruff, and he cleared his throat.

"We?"

"My sister, Tam, and I."

"I didn't know you had a sister." She brushed her hair away from her face and turned in her seat as much as the seat belt would allow, so he had a better view of her face. Her gaze was filled with casual interest.

"She's just finishing college. In the fall she'll start med school."

"A doctor! That's very impressive. You must have special genes in your family or something. Were your parents Christians?"

"Yes." Todd paused as he navigated the turn off the highway. "I remember my mother praying over us in bed every night, that we would follow Christ every day in our lives and that he would use us in a special way to further his kingdom."

Kate smiled. "Well, he's certainly answered her prayers. A pastor and a doctor."

Todd squeezed her hand. She hadn't said the words aloud, but something told him she was cutting herself down again— this time by what she wasn't saying. "It isn't what you do for a living, Kate. It's how you do it."

She quietly withdrew her hand from his and gazed out the window.

"What about you?" he asked. "Any brothers or sisters?"

"Nope. I'm an only child. And now it's just me and my mom. That's why I can't understand—"

"Why she wants to move into Roseborough," he finished for her.

She nodded miserably.

They drove in silence for a minute as Todd sorted through his thoughts. "Maybe this is something she needs to do," he said at last. "Roseborough is a great place for retired people, Kate. She'll never be bored."

"Todd, she has MS," Kate blurted, suddenly angry.

He blew out a breath. That did put a different spin on things. The whole picture was coming into focus. "I see."

"Do you?" She pulled her knees into her chest and wrapped her arms around her legs.

He glanced at her and smiled. "They have nurses on call twenty-four hours a day."

"So my mother says."

"It won't be the same as you caring for her."

"No, it won't." Bitterness lined every word.

"But it's what she wants."

Kate was silent for so long he wondered if she'd heard, when she finally answered. "I know. I have to let her go."

His heart clenched in his chest, but he forced himself to breathe through it. "Can I help?"

"You already have." Her smile was like sunshine piercing through the clouds. "Who else could I whine to and get away with it?"

He chuckled. "That's what I get paid for."

"Oh, right. I forgot. I hired you as my personal shrink."

"It's no problem, Kate."

"And helping me find a place to live is certainly beyond the call of duty, however you call it," she teased.

"It's called being a friend. No charge." He flashed her his

cheesiest grin. "We're almost to the place I told you about."

"Oh, good. I'm sure I'll feel better once I know for sure I have someplace lined up when the time comes to make the big, bad move."

"Sure you will. In the meantime, why don't you see if you can't find a few other complexes for us to visit. We have the whole afternoon, so we can probably hit most of them."

Minutes later, Todd pulled into the complex where he lived. A rental sign with directions to see the manager in the office was posted in the yard across the drive from his own townhouse. He parked his truck and leaned his forearms on the steering wheel.

Kate sat quietly, staring at her hands clasped in her lap, making no move to open the door.

He took a deep breath. "Why don't you go in and inquire? I'll wait for you here."

If he walked into that office with Kate, his cover would be blown to smithereens. He'd been around the office enough for the office manager to know him on sight. And since he still didn't know what had possessed him to bring her home, he thought it would be better to avoid the obvious. He didn't know why he didn't just blurt out the truth, but something inside held him back.

He waited while Kate went into the office, juggling his feelings for her in his mind, feeling very much as if he were digging himself into a deeper hole than he'd already managed. He needed to put everything in perspective, and quickly.

Like tell her he lived in this complex, for starters. And while he was at it, he might as well mention that he worked at Roseborough. And just to make absolutely certain she'd never speak to him again as long as they both should live, he might as well admit that he was attracted to her. That despite the fact that she was his employer and he wanted to keep his job, he wanted to pursue a relationship with her that went beyond business.

He thumped his palm on the steering wheel and swung himself out of the pickup.

How quickly he forgot. Kate meddled with his insides, making him want what he'd planned to put off for now. What he thought God required of him—to stay away from getting involved in a relationship.

He wasn't being fair to Kate to so much as consider pursuing anything with her. What kind of life could he offer her? He didn't have a *real* job. He could barely meet his own expenses, especially since he was trying to help his sister out. Providing for a wife was out of the question.

Kate exited the office, dangling a key from her fingers and breaking abruptly into his thoughts. "The manager said to let myself in."

Todd didn't return her cheerful smile. In fact, he was scowling, his dark eyebrows puckered together.

She looked around to see what had changed his mood, but the parking lot was quiet. Only a few cars were parked in the lot, and there were no people around. The only movement was within a small community of prairie dogs on the edge of the lot and a couple of kids playing basketball in one corner.

"Get in a fight with a prairie dog?" she asked, gesturing to the furry creatures.

His eyes widened in surprise, then the lines on his face eased and he chuckled. "No. Just feeling grouchy. Ready to see the place?"

"Answering a question with a question is a clear sign of a

man trying to hide something. What are you trying to hide, Todd Jensen?"

Or not.

What she meant to be a joke sparked to life with an electric tension that sizzled in the air between them.

His jaw tightened, and he looked away. Then his mouth twitched into a slow smile. "Yeah, I'm just a bundle of mystery." His normally liquid brown eyes shaded into muddy pools.

Are all men this polar, or just Todd? And they say women are moody! Kate shrugged and whirled away from him. He could stand there all day if he wanted to. She had a townhouse to look at.

She took a deep, fortifying breath and turned the key in the lock. As the door swung open, she felt as if the door were opening to a whole new stage of life. The hair stood on the back of her neck, as if a wisp of cold wind brushed down her spine.

But when she stepped inside, her heart warmed at once. The large, open living room welcomed her, and the sunshine peering through the windows acted as treasured solace to her quivering soul.

The house faced south, she noticed immediately, so the apartment would bask in sunshine throughout the day. Sunshine was a must for Kate.

She stepped into the kitchen, which was done in a cheery floral-patterned wallpaper with light almond appliances. A small window stood over the sink, giving her a peek onto a decent-sized back porch and the tennis courts beyond. Frilly white lace curtains and a couple of well-placed house plants were all she needed to complete the picture.

To make it home.

There was even a dishwasher, a luxury she'd been without

the past few years. It would be nice not to have to do dishes by hand.

Todd cleared his throat behind her. She tossed a glance over her shoulder to where he stood, arms crossed, leaning his bulky shoulder against the kitchen door frame.

"What do you think?" His voice was low, and as rich as the thick chocolate carpeting at his feet.

What did she think? That this was exactly what she hadn't even known she'd been looking for? That it was perfect?

That it was home?

She held up her index finger, gesturing for him to wait. She hadn't seen the upstairs yet.

She took the stairs two at a time and quickly scanned the rest of the townhouse. A good-sized bathroom with a large whirlpool bathtub awaited her. When she discovered a walk-in closet in the large master bedroom, she voiced her pleasure aloud in an unfettered exclamation of joy.

Pure and simple luxury, and well within her price range. Absolutely amazing!

Todd was amazing. He'd selected a townhouse at random, and it turned out to be exactly what she wanted. She could have looked at a thousand models, yet he led her to the perfect one on the first try. How had he known, when she hadn't known herself?

"This is it!" she exclaimed, fluttering back down the stairs.

Todd chuckled. He had moved to the living room. For lack of furniture, he'd sprawled on the floor, his weight propped on one elbow, his head in his palm. "Don't you want a little more information about it before you make a decision?"

Kate felt the heat warm on her cheeks. Perhaps she was swept up and carried away by the moment. She hadn't actually looked at any other complexes.

"Like what? I've seen the house, and the price is right." Flopping down Indian-style on the carpet next to Todd, she rested her chin on her fists.

She could—probably *should*—spend the day looking at every townhouse on the market. It was the sensible, practical, Kate thing to do. But what if she went to look elsewhere and someone else snapped this gem up? She was already beginning to think of it as hers, mentally planning all the changes that would make it home.

For once in her life, she didn't want to be practical. Choosing a home was a matter of the heart. And her heart was saying stay.

"You should consider the amenities. This is a particularly nice complex," he said, ticking a list off on his fingers. "I'm sure you saw the tennis courts. There's a swimming pool. And they have a spectacular weight room." Rolling to a sitting position, he struck a pose and flexed his biceps.

"I think you'll find this place to have everything you need. Or want," he added quickly.

She narrowed her eyes on him. "Sounds like you're trying to sell me on the place, not warn me off."

His face turned a glowing shade of red, and he thrust his hand through his hair, spiking the ends.

"Maybe I am," he said huskily, then cleared his throat. "They keep the swimming pool so warm it's almost a hot tub. A real treat after a long day's work."

"And exactly how do you know all this?" She suspected she already knew the answer, but the urge to torment him won out. Her heart pounded double time as she waited for his answer.

He cleared his throat again, looking very much like a cornered rabbit, glancing right and left, trying to find somewhere to hide. "I...er, live here," he finally admitted, refusing to meet her eyes. "Just across the drive."

"Todd Andrew Jensen!" Kate exclaimed, pulling his middle name from the recesses of her mind, where she'd conveniently tucked it after perusing his résumé. "Why didn't you tell me that in the first place?"

"I didn't want to influence you?"

Laughter bubbled up in her chest, escaping her lips despite her best efforts to the contrary. "In other words, the privilege of living in the same complex with my wedding-chapel chaplain should be considered at the top of the amenities list?"

His laughter followed hers, deep from the confines of his chest. "More like I thought you'd be inclined to run in the opposite direction and never give this place a chance."

How wrong can a man be? She sat immobile as her heart rode the surf of her emotions.

Their eyes met and silence reigned. He reached a tentative hand toward her, brushing her cheek lightly with the pad of his thumb. Her heart was pounding with such fierce irregularity that she was certain he could hear it from where he sat.

His eyes, those speaking, warm brown pools, swirled with unnamed emotion, and Kate forgot to breathe.

"Have dinner with me." The request was whispered so lightly that she thought she might have imagined it, except that he continued. "Tonight."

Her heart spun and dropped into the pit of her stomach, where it continued to zip around like a jumping-jack firecracker on the Fourth of July, screaming for her to answer *yes!* to his query.

"But not as my boss, Kate." He dropped his hand and ruffled

it through his hair, his eyes never leaving hers. "As my friend."

Her swirling insides stopped abruptly as the dense lead of reality coated them.

As his friend.

Why did he have to ruin the moment by asking the impossible?

She swallowed hard, trying to rein in her feelings, forcing to the surface the veneer of control that had seen her through so many crises in her past.

This, she thought miserably, *might well turn out to be the worst yet.* Even so, she tipped her chin in the air and met Todd's seeking gaze head-on.

"No." She was surprised that her voice didn't waver. She might be quivering on the inside, but he would never know. "I don't think that's a good idea."

His eyes widened in surprise. She watched a flicker of emotion pass through them before he lowered his eyelids slightly, his long, dark lashes shading his gaze. His lips thinned to a hard, straight line.

"I see," he said gruffly.

No, you don't see at all. That's the point.

She clenched her fists against the notion to shake him until he *did* see the truth—that Katie the Whale was falling head over heels for a man she didn't deserve and could never have even if she wanted to.

The realization smacked her in the face, and with it came the instinctive urge to protect herself. She didn't dare get any closer to him. His overture of friendship was more than she could handle right now, maybe ever. The best thing she could do—for both of them—was to make a fast and furious retreat.

"I'm going back to the office to put a down payment on this place," she said, her voice rough and gravelly.

He didn't rise with her, or so much glance at her. She couldn't tell if he was breathing, so still he sat, staring at his hands, as if the answers to the world's problems were written there.

He wasn't even going to respond.

Rejection flowed through her chest. A bitter laugh threatened to escape her throat. Deep down in her heart, she wanted him to beg. To profess his undying love for her and sweep her off her feet. *What a joke.*

And oh, the irony of it. She'd just rejected him, yet she felt like the one abruptly abandoned.

She'd never been good at the silent treatment. "Lock up behind you, will you?" she mumbled in a monotone.

"I'll wait for you in the truck," he said as she walked out the door.

Dunderhead, his sister would have called him. *Blunderbuss. Nitwit.*

He had a few names to add to that label. *Idiot. Jerk. Fool.* He pounded his fist against the steering wheel, frustration seething from his bones. He knew he couldn't cross that line between employer and friend without creating enormous complications—problems he was much better without. He knew Kate kept a brick wall between herself and the world. He was trained as a pastor, for all the good it did him. She couldn't be expected to trust him after such a short time.

Trust was earned. It came slowly, like snow melting in the sunshine. And he, like a fool, had just tried to swing in with all the grace of Tarzan and break down the wall in one fell swoop. What a jerk.

Oh, God. What have I done?

He leaned his forehead against his fist on the steering wheel, pushing hard against his temple where his pulse threatened to burst.

He would lose his job, let Tam down. Worse, he'd lose the thin threads of friendship that connected him to Kate.

Confusion stabbed through his gut like a dagger, and he gritted his teeth against pain that was so intense it was almost physical. He'd been so sure he was meant to be single, that God had given him work to do that a woman could not share. It wasn't fair to drag a wife into it. He couldn't provide for her or protect her. He had nothing to offer. What kind of a husband could he be?

But knowing Kate had changed everything. She stirred feelings in him he'd thought never to experience, and it scared him. He'd always been able to keep a tight rein on his emotions, never mind his baser instincts. But Kate wiped that away with a single smile. No amount of conviction or determination could make his fickle body, much less his heart, understand.

To give them beauty for ashes, the oil of joy for mourning, the garment of praise for the spirit of heaviness.

Isaiah's words pierced into his consciousness, and he grappled for the ending of the verse.

That they may be called trees of righteousness, the planting of the Lord, that He may be glorified.

He let out the breath he'd unconsciously been holding, feeling the effect of God's Word like balm to his spirit.

That was it, then. God could turn his mangled attempt at reaching out into something good, could restore his focus on the Lord Jesus Christ. God could take the ashes he'd created and turn them into something beautiful.

He let out a breath of relief. Thank God he was calling the shots, and that even Todd's own stumbling and stalling could be made into something beautiful when put into God's hands.

Maybe, Lord willing, he could still help the woman he'd so foolishly managed to push away. And if he couldn't, at least he could rest in the knowledge that Jesus would be there to do what he couldn't.

He closed his eyes and prayed for God to be glorified, and didn't notice Kate approaching the truck until the passenger door opened and she quietly slipped in.

He opened his eyes to find her sitting with her hands clasped tightly in her lap, tears running silently down her cheeks. Instinctively he put his arm around her shoulders and drew her into his embrace. It was what he had wanted to do from the moment he'd first seen her, and it felt every bit as good and right as he'd known it would. His chest filled with the need to protect her from whatever was hurting her, to soothe her wounds. He stroked her hair, silky beneath his touch and smelling of a fresh summer breeze.

"Kate," he began hesitantly, but she cut him off, shaking her head almost violently. He felt her tremble in his arms, and he tightened his hold on her.

She raised her face so their gazes locked. "I'm sorry I'm sniveling," she said, her full bottom lip quivering. "It…it's so stupid! I can't even believe I'm crying about this." She attempted a quivering smile. "You'd think I'd be used to it by now. It's the story of my life."

Todd smiled gently and wiped the tears from her cheeks with his index finger. She was obviously distressed, but she was trying to smile. He couldn't recall ever having met a woman with the inner strength Kate Logan showed on a regular basis. What other woman would put aside her own plans, her own dreams and goals, to care for her mother?

She had a successful business of her own, built with her

own hard work. And she'd managed to make it into a ministry, every bit as important as the job he did, in its own way. He wasn't sure she was aware how many lives she touched with her efforts and her natural tendency to reach out, sympathizing with everyone's pain.

She was amazing. But she was unhappy.

What could make this beautiful woman so miserable? *Father,* he thought, repeating a prayer he'd said often the past few weeks, *help me to reach her with your love.*

"What's wrong?" he asked when she remained silent.

She laughed weakly. "By the time I got back to the office with the key, someone else had phoned in a down payment on the place." She stopped and hiccuped a breath. "I guess I'm still homeless after all."

Seven

Monday, Kate dragged her feet in getting to the office, managing to putter around the house until early afternoon. She felt like an absolute idiot, bursting into tears over the loss of a townhouse that wasn't hers to begin with. How stupid could she be?

And of course it had to be in front of Todd. As always, he had been perfect. He knew what to say, how to respond. If only she could learn to do what came naturally to him. How many people would she be able to help with that innate knowledge.

He had given her absolutely no reason to believe his attention went beyond pastoral, though her heart continued to whisper the suggestion that perhaps there was more to it. And though she tried not to dwell on it, she had enjoyed being held in his arms. But his tender comfort had merely amplified her feelings. She determined to keep him at arm's length.

Unable to stall any longer, she walked down Thomas's garden path and into the basement office. Might as well face the music and get it over with.

She expected three curious, concerned faces to greet her, knowing if Todd had said a word to either Thomas or Elizabeth, they'd feel obligated to share their opinions on the subject. Her friends never had been the type to mind their own business, especially where she was concerned.

To her surprise, the office hummed with busy activity. No one appeared to notice her entrance at all. Thomas and Elizabeth stood in the far corner, arranging wedding photographs into an album for display, arguing vigorously over the placement of a picture.

Kate smiled. Those two couldn't do anything without arguing.

Todd was seated at her desk. Her desk! What was he doing…besides invading her space again.

He swung around in the swivel chair and grinned up at her. "Sorry. Haven't got that much of my own to do this morning, so I thought I'd pitch in here."

It was on the tip of her tongue to tell him to kindly keep his help to himself, but instead she sighed. "Sorry I'm late. What have you accomplished?"

He swiveled back around to the desk, where her papers were piled in neat stacks. "I found the form letter you use for general inquiries and copied them for all of these." He patted a large pile of envelopes. "All I need is your signature, and I can stuff, lick, and stamp. Oh, and I sorted your mail. Here's the pile you need to respond to; the rest of this stuff is file thirteen I think.

"Don't worry," he continued when she opened her mouth to speak. "I didn't throw anything away before you had a chance to look at it."

Heat rose to her cheeks, a mixture of anger and embarrassment. She felt as if he'd just unearthed her darkest secrets, meddled with her private possessions, instead of simply taken care of some paperwork. "I didn't hire you to be my secretary, Todd."

"I can't preach all the time," he teased, "so I might as well make myself useful. I thought if I could save you some time and a headache or two, all the better."

"Yes, but—"

"I don't mind. Really. Besides, I'm just fulfilling your advertisement. 'Team player needed to work closely with the wedding coordinator.' Remember?"

She felt warmth shimmy down her spine at having her words thrown back at her. She didn't guess when she was writing them that they'd rise up to haunt her.

The phone rang, and Elizabeth answered. Her cheery greeting turned quickly to a look of concern, and the others gathered around her. She made several conciliatory noises from the back of her throat, then asked the caller to hold.

"What is it?" Kate asked calmly. "Do we have a problem?"

Elizabeth nodded gravely. "I'll say. Lynda McMahon and Joe just split up. Permanently."

Kate felt the muscles in her shoulder blades tighten across her back. It wasn't the first time a couple had decided to call it quits before the wedding day, especially after the premarital counseling her consulting service required. It was amazing what couples neglected to reveal about themselves until put under pressure.

But not Lynda and Joe. She'd been so certain about them. A young Christian couple with their feet on the ground and their dreams in the air. If Lynda and Joe couldn't work it out, what kind of hope did that leave for the rest of the world? What hope did it leave for a woman like her? Her mood dropped like the temperature after a Colorado sunset.

There were other matters to consider, of course. A called-off wedding always meant a severe financial loss, as Wedding Works usually ended up eating some if not all of the prepaid expenses.

"We've already picked up the silk flowers and ordered the wedding cake," Thomas said, reading her thoughts.

She slid a glance at Todd, who smiled encouragement at her. "Did she say what the problem is?"

"It's a doozy," said Elizabeth, shaking her head. "Children. A week before the wedding, and they finally decide to talk about whether or not they want kids."

Todd reached for the phone. "That's what you hired me for." He punched the red button on the telephone. "Lynda?" he said gently into the receiver.

His voice was low, rich, and compassionate, and it warmed Kate's heart. He'd used that tone with her yesterday in the truck. His pastor's voice. A sliver of disappointment pierced through her, but she mentally shoved the feeling aside.

"This is Father Todd Jensen. Can you tell me what's wrong?"

Apparently she could, and she did. Kate could hear the muffled wailing from where she stood.

Todd was silent, inserting only an occasional *uh-huh* or grunt of understanding. Kate and the others went back to work in Thomas's corner, discreetly trying not to listen to their chaplain at work.

After a few minutes Todd said good-bye, punched another number, and carried on a quick, low-pitched conversation. When he replaced the receiver in the cradle, he smiled broadly and crossed his arms over the broad expanse of his chest. He looked, Kate thought, just the tiniest bit smug.

"Hope your schedule is clear, boss. We have a meeting with Lynda and Joe in an hour."

"*We* do?"

"Of course. I promised Lynda you'd be there. To lend moral support and a feminine perspective, if you know what I mean."

"No, I don't know what you mean," she complained good-naturedly. "Care to fill me in on the details, or am I supposed to wing it?" She didn't know what she was being so short-tempered about. Todd had stepped in and proven what a good choice she'd made in a chaplain. She should be elated.

It was just that…everything came so easily to him.

He ducked down behind the back of her desk and reappeared with several giant three-ring notebooks. Each one was at least four inches thick and brimming with different colored papers.

He used his hip to clear a space on the desk and set the notebooks down with a satisfying smack. "This," he said proudly, "is the soon-to-be-famous Jensen Premarital Counseling Program."

"And I have an hour to memorize it?" she asked weakly. How could anyone find that much to say about marital counseling?

Todd waved his hand in a dismissive gesture. "Of course not. Only pages 214 through 349."

Her jaw dropped in astonishment, causing Thomas and Elizabeth to break into laughter.

"Just kidding," Todd assured her with a grin.

Kate pulled the top notebook toward her and cracked it open, shaking her head in disbelief as she thumbed through the pages. It was a counseling program, all right. Pages of neatly typed research and case studies, carefully numbered and indexed. It was a work of art; that's what it was.

"What is this, the ten-year plan? Most of our couples want to marry within the year, you know."

Todd snatched the notebook away from her and hid it behind his back in a protective gesture. His face looked grim, but laughter was shining from his dark eyes. "These are just for *my* reference. The actual program is six weeks."

Elizabeth tapped the top of the pile of remaining notebooks. "Anything in here for children fighting about having children?"

"Pages 214 through 349." He looked down his nose at Kate. "And you thought I was kidding."

"Did you actually write this tome?" she asked, her voice betraying her awe.

"Every word." He grinned widely. "Well, not every word. I borrowed some from my research. I've been working on this puppy for two years."

"Well, I apparently hired the right man for the job. I had no idea you had this much interest in premarital counseling."

"A funny hobby, if you ask me," muttered Thomas, eyeing the volumes with evident distaste.

Elizabeth swatted him in the arm. "At least Todd has a hobby, you miserable excuse for a human being."

Todd cleared his throat. "It's not—er, a hobby, really. It's my doctoral treatise."

"You're getting your doctorate?" the two women declared simultaneously.

Thomas groaned and turned back to his photography table.

"Oh, hush, Thomas. You're just jealous," Kate teased.

"Am not," Thomas muttered, ducking as if in anticipation of flying projectiles.

"Stop picking on the poor guy," Todd said, laughing deeply. "Getting a doctorate isn't all it's cracked up to be. Thankfully I'm finished with the course work. All I have left to do is a six-week stint in Brighton, and it's a done deal."

"Brighton as in England?" Kate asked, envy fluttering through her stomach. She'd always wanted to travel.

"Sounds like an awfully lonely place to be going by your-self," Elizabeth purred, making the hair stand up on Kate's neck.

"Would you look at the time," Kate said loudly, thrusting her wrist in front of Todd's nose. "We'd best be off. Where did you say we were meeting?"

"I didn't," he said, lowering her arm so he could meet her gaze. "But you're right. We should be going."

There, she'd cut Elizabeth off before she'd done any harm.

Todd wouldn't know what she'd been hinting at. He didn't know Elizabeth as she did.

"And Elizabeth," Todd continued, his mouth tipping into a grin. "You're right, too. I'll give some serious thought to getting myself married before I go."

"A pizza parlor?" Kate clutched at Todd's upper arm and hissed in his ear. "This poor couple has to try to resolve their differences in a pizza parlor? Todd, what were you thinking?"

He smiled to himself as he walked around the truck to open the door for her. He liked having her close to him. So much so, in fact, that as they walked across the parking lot, he reached his arm around to clasp her around the waist under the guise of whispering in her ear.

"We're talking about a stubborn male, here," he reminded her. "Trust me on this—food is a good thing."

Kate appeared to consider his statement, softly chewing on her bottom lip. "Mmm. You've got a point there." She nudged him with her elbow. "I hate to be the one to blast a big hole in your little theory. You might be forced to rewrite that doctoral thesis of yours."

"Hole?" he protested, tightening his hold on her waist. "What hole?"

"What if she's the one being stubborn? It's been known to happen, you know."

"Do I know it...ow!" he exclaimed as she elbowed him again, harder this time. "I meant my sister, present company definitely excepted." He opened the door of the pizza parlor and held it for her.

"Sure, you did," said Kate with a laugh. "By the way, what did you say to Joe to get him to agree to meet with us?"

He smiled and gave her his best mysterious look.

"Todd…" she warned.

"Okay, okay! I'd like to keep the rest of my ribs, thank you."

"Kate!" Lynda called from a corner table.

Not secluded, Todd noted, but as private as a pizza parlor would allow. Perfect for what he had in mind.

Kate moved toward the table, but he held her back by the elbow. "I offered to buy," he whispered, causing her to swallow a laugh.

For a woman as normally reserved as Kate, she knew when to reach out to someone, moving straight to Lynda's side and putting her arms around her.

Todd entertained a distinctly unpastoral desire to slam his fist into Joe's swarthy face when he showed up. While his mind acknowledged the fact that Joe had could just as well be the "innocent party" here, his gut said Joe had made a woman cry. Not just any woman, but the woman he intended to marry. And that made Todd mad.

Reality was probably something in between, he acknowledged. Arguments were rarely one sided. He was more than likely dealing with two stubborn individuals. It was a touchy situation, but sensitive cases were his specialty.

The first order of business was pizza. "Shall we order?" he asked, gesturing Joe into the booth across from Lynda. Let the guy sit across from his intended and have to make eye contact…rather than body contact that might prove adverse to the situation. Of course, Lynda could still land Joe a swift kick in the shin, but Todd hoped it wouldn't come to that.

"What kind of pizza do we want?" Kate asked a little too brightly.

Her eyes were glassy in the dim light of the parlor, probably brought on by a combination of anxiety and adrenaline. He wanted to reach out to her, to let her know he was feeling the same way, but he suspected playing footsie under the table would not rank high with her right now.

"I like sausage and extra cheese," he said instead.

"Make it pepperoni and we've got a deal," Kate said, the light squeak in her voice betraying her discomfort.

"Done," he agreed easily, thinking he'd agree to just about anything when Kate flashed those huge amber eyes on him.

"Joe? Lynda?" she said. "What about you?"

"Sausage and mushroom," Lynda said.

"Canadian bacon and pineapple," Joe said at the same time.

Todd swallowed his breath. This wasn't a good start. He was about to intervene when Joe snaked his hand across the table and grasped Lynda's. Surprisingly, she didn't snatch it away. In fact, their eyes met and locked, and he had the distinct impression that the world had just faded to the two individuals.

Perhaps things weren't so bad after all.

Lynda drew her breath in sharply, and Joe licked his lips.

"Canadian bacon and pineapple," Joe said, his voice raspy.

"But Joe—" Lynda protested.

"Canadian bacon and pineapple," he said again.

Selfish lout, Todd thought. He had planned to take Joe aside and let Kate deal with Lynda, but now he wished it were okay for him to let Kate have the pleasure. He wasn't sure he had the patience for a man who forced his own wishes on the woman he supposedly loved.

"That was a very sweet gesture, Joe," Kate said quietly.

Todd almost exclaimed aloud. His blood roared in his ears. Of all the ridiculous things to say! He was opening his mouth to protest when he felt Kate nudge his leg beneath the table.

Don't you get it? her expression said.

The tears ran freely down Lynda's face. "Oh, Joe, I do love you!"

Todd's first thought was that the whole world had gone crazy. His second thought was that maybe he should have let Joe sit by Lynda after all.

"All's well that ends well, I suppose," Kate said with a tired sigh. Every muscle in her body ached, as if she'd been running a marathon instead of attending a counseling session. She leaned her head back until it met the upholstery of the truck seat and closed her eyes.

She had a new respect for Todd. In the back of her mind, she had to admit she'd thought pastors had a pretty plush, out-in-the-spotlight kind of life. She'd only seen the preaching and teaching aspects of a pastor's work. The rest of the time she supposed he spent with his nose buried in some dusty old theological volume, preparing for speaking once again.

Now she was seeing the other side—the tasks pastors quietly performed but didn't talk about. Like counseling, for instance. It wasn't as simple as it seemed.

She and Todd had spent three hours with two people who obviously wanted to be together yet had a host of issues to weed through in order to be reunited.

"How did you get Joe to concede?" she asked, voicing her thoughts. "On the kid issue, I mean, not the pizza. Nothing short of a miracle, if you ask me."

Todd chuckled and furrowed his brow, shaking his head fervently. "Let's leave the miracle-working to Jesus, shall we?"

"I just meant that—"

"The Holy Spirit was definitely lending us a hand," he finished for her. "Amen to that."

"Yes," she agreed dryly, torn between a smile and a frown. "Amen to that."

He slid a glance at her she couldn't read, and she returned it with wide eyes and raised brows. "What?"

"You're pretty incredible," he said, the timbre of his voice changing to a low rasp.

"Me?" Kate exclaimed, her heart pounding double time in her ears. Waves of emotion rushed over her at the compliment, and she could feel herself blushing fiercely.

"Yes, you," he repeated, his attention on the mousetrap turn he was executing to get them on the highway. "Why do you sound so surprised?"

"I thought we'd already established that it was the Holy Spirit doing the work there today."

"My point exactly. You allow yourself to be used by God. You reached out when you saw a person in need. There are a lot of people who would walk right on by, you know."

Her heart swelled into her throat, cutting off her breath. She started to deny her part as inconsequential, but Todd cut her off.

"It *isn't* nothing, and you know it. Most wedding consulting businesses are all about gowns and lace and invitations. You've gone and made it a business about people! It takes a special kind of person to do that."

"I knew right away that you were the kind of man to step in and reach out a helping hand," Kate said in a transparent attempt to change the subject. Enough about herself.

"I'm in ministry, yes," Todd agreed. "And I love what I do. But I'm not a natural. I've got the desire in here." He thumped himself on the chest. "But it doesn't automatically work itself out to helping people the way it does with you. I have to force it a bit."

"Like you had to force Joe to capitulate?" she asked, trying to lighten a mood. "What did you do when you took him into the game room, twist his arm behind his back until he pleaded for mercy?"

"Of course not," he said, looking offended. "I wouldn't resort to such base tactics…unless it suited my purposes. I can wrestle if I have to."

He waggled his eyebrows at her, and she laughed. The thought of being pinned by Todd wasn't all that unpleasant.

"As it turned out, I didn't have to do much but listen," he continued. "Most counseling is just listening. Letting someone know you care."

"Lynda was ready to make up with Joe, too. Even if it meant giving up the thought of ever having children."

"That wouldn't have worked," he adamantly stated. "Children are one of those issues a couple shouldn't compromise on. Not when you're talking a lifetime."

Kate tended to agree and wondered if Todd wanted children. It was on the tip of her tongue to ask him, but she couldn't find the words.

Being an only child, she longed for a large family, three or four children at least. But if Katie the Whale didn't scare off a man, her visions of home and hearth certainly would. She chuckled under her breath.

Todd smiled in response. "Joe was afraid to admit he wanted kids," he continued. "All he could think about was the responsibility. He didn't think they should talk about it until they'd managed to buy a house, save enough for four years of college per child and then some—you know, typical guy stuff."

"If a couple waited until they could afford to have kids, they'd never have them!"

"Exactly what I told him. And then, of course, I reminded him of the son that would carry on the family name, and the little daughter, the spitting image of Lynda, all gussied up in curls and pearls. The center of her daddy's heart."

When Todd said "daddy," Kate's breath caught. How easy it was to picture him bouncing a baby on his knee. A tiny baby girl with dark locks like her daddy's.

But of course it wouldn't be her baby Todd would be bouncing. Far safer to pop her own bubble than to float around until she met something sharp.

"Lynda said—" her throat caught again and she stopped to clear it—"she has so much love for Joe that she sometimes feels like it's overflowing—that it'll burst if she doesn't find a way to use it. She thinks that is what having children is about. The overflow of a love between a couple."

Todd reached across the cab and took her hand, squeezing it lightly. "That sounds like true love to me," he said, his voice hoarse. "God's love flowing through two people into their children."

Kate was silent. She couldn't speak if she wanted to, her throat was so tight. Her lungs felt ready to burst, but she couldn't coax herself to breathe. Time was suspended, and it felt like just the two of them in the world.

Suddenly there was a loud popping noise, and the truck veered sharply to the right. Todd pulled his hand back to the wheel and turned them straight just before they rolled into the low, grassy gully at the side of the highway.

Kate grabbed for the dashboard to keep from banging her head on the ceiling. The truck was equipped with a roll bar, but she hoped they wouldn't have the opportunity to use it.

Todd mumbled under his breath. *Cursing or praying?* Kate wondered.

"A flat," he said loud enough for her to hear. "What am I supposed to do with a flat tire?"

Change it seemed the obvious answer, but Kate wasn't about to suggest it. Todd was scowling so deeply that his eyebrows were a straight, dark line low on his forehead.

"Do you have a jack?" she asked instead, glad she was in jeans and a T-shirt instead of the dress she'd almost donned that morning. "If you get the spare, I'll start pulling the flat off."

She opened her door and had one foot on the ground when Todd answered. "Oh, no, you don't. You are not changing my flat tire."

She snorted and lifted an eyebrow. "I'm not playing helpless heroine if that's what you're waiting for," she said dryly. *"Hay-ulp! Hay-ulp!* just doesn't cut it for me."

She didn't wait for him to answer but swung down from the truck and walked around to the back. She didn't see a spare or jack in the back of the truck, so she resolved herself to the inevitable crawl underneath.

It was a good thing that she was an only child, she reflected wryly. Her father hadn't had a son to teach to tinker with cars, so he'd taught Kate. And while she wasn't a grease monkey by any means of the word, she did enjoy keeping her car in tip-top running condition. She could be found from time to time under the hood of her Honda. And she *could* change a tire. Even a truck tire.

She could see the spare tire tucked just under the back end, and she suspected the jack was suspended there as well.

"I don't suppose you have an old blanket or something?"

she asked Todd, who had barreled out of the truck after her.

"What do you need a blanket for?" he asked through his teeth.

It didn't take a genius to see that the woman was showing him up, and he didn't like the feeling. But he wasn't sure he could catch up in this arena. Cars weren't really his forte any more than baseball was.

Sure, he'd changed a tire now and again but not on this truck. And the last thing he wanted to do was to bumble around with Kate watching.

"Well, I don't exactly *need* a blanket," she amended, too cheerfully, he thought, "but it would be a little easier on my back and knees if I had something to lie on."

"Oh." He walked back to the cab and reached behind the seat for the red plaid woolen blanket he kept there.

Her eyes lit up as he returned and offered the blanket. She was enjoying this; she really was. He felt his dander rising like a cat with his hair rubbed the wrong way.

"A picnic blanket!" she exclaimed. "Great idea, but we've already eaten. I don't know about you, but I'm stuffed from the pizza."

Still sulking over his flat tire, it took him a moment to respond. "It's for your back."

Her eyes warmed with laughter. "You don't mind if I get it dirty?"

"Humph." He waved away her concern.

The point was that he should be the one getting dirty, crawling under his truck for who knew what purpose, instead of her. But she wasn't about to concede that point, he knew, so he crossed his arms over his chest and mentally licked his wounded pride.

He heard clanging and a loud *ouch!* Moments later, Kate slid from beneath the truck.

She ran a greasy hand down the front of her T-shirt, leaving several black streaks in its wake. "I can't get the spare off. The bolt is too tight. I think it's a job for Muscle Man."

Nabbing the opportunity to balm his pride, Todd rolled to the ground and pushed himself under the truck, paying no heed to the blanket Kate had used. A thistle bit into his shoulder, and he wondered at the wisdom of his rash action. Maybe she'd been right about the blanket.

He gritted his teeth and slid further, ignoring the sound of tearing cotton. One of his good clerical shirts. It figured. He only had two.

He reached the tire, and it came off easily in his hands, leaving him to wonder if Kate really had had the trouble she'd claimed or if this was a blatant plot to restore him to good humor. If it was the latter, he decided magnanimously, he'd better be sure her efforts didn't go to waste.

It took only minutes for them to change the tire. They really did make a good team, he reflected. Enough alike to complement each other, yet different enough to sharpen one another as well.

And Kate wasn't afraid to get her hands dirty. He could marry a woman like that. Struck by the thought, he helped her back into the cab, taking a good, long look at her as he did.

She was adorably messy. Her once white T-shirt was smudged with streaks of dirt and grease. Her short brown hair hung around the sweet, soft contours of her face in wild disarray. She met his gaze expectantly from her perch in the cab. It would take only the merest effort to close the distance between them, to brush his mouth across her full, sweet red lips.

Tension escalated between them. He could see the shuttered

look in her eye, knew she could tell what he was thinking.

And she didn't move away.

So he did.

He broke their electrifying eye contact and ran for his side of the cab. He couldn't kiss her now, no matter how much he wanted to. Whether or not he chose to do so in the future was open to debate. But he made himself a vow as he pulled up into the cab and fastened his seat belt. He would not kiss Kate until he could make her the promise she deserved.

If she were another woman, he wouldn't have hesitated, but he wouldn't trifle with Kate's feelings. She'd been hurt, and he wouldn't hurt her worse by making unspoken promises he couldn't keep.

He drove her home without a word. When they arrived at her house, she mumbled good night and bolted for the door.

Running from him, no doubt. Until he worked through the jumbled mess that had become his brain, he would not move forward in his relationship with her. She was too good a woman to be toyed with and then dropped when the time came for him to take up one of those tough ministries God called people to from time to time.

Yet if a woman existed who could accompany him on his missions of mercy, it was Kate. She was—incredible. Dauntless. And scared to death of something.

He would put a lid on his feelings until he knew for certain what he was already beginning to suspect.

That Kate Logan was the woman he'd been waiting his whole life to meet.

Kate closed the door softly so as not to wake her mother. If only it were as easy to close the door to her heart.

He'd been going to kiss her. She knew it. His eyes held nothing back. She'd seen the way they clouded as his gaze dropped to her lips.

Then he'd pulled away.

Why? Why wouldn't he kiss her when he clearly wanted to?

Katie the whale. The taunt echoed through her head, but she pushed it away.

She should have kissed him; that's what she should have done. She had imagined their first kiss a hundred times. As tender and gentle as the man himself.

Oh, who was she trying to kid? She wouldn't ever find the nerve to kiss Todd. Thinking about it was only setting herself up for a fall, which was exactly what she was doing with every passing moment.

She recalled one time as a child when she'd begged her father to take her on the roller coaster at the fair. He'd tried to explain what she was asking to do, but she was a stubborn little girl, the center of her father's heart, and he'd eventually relented. It was only after the coaster was in motion that she realized she really didn't want to be where she was. But it was too late to stop the ride.

She felt like that now. Despite her best defenses, she'd fallen in love, and there wasn't a thing she could think of to do about it, no way to get off the ride.

Except to pray. The words whispered through her mind. She could pray at least. Or maybe it was the *most* she could do. If anyone could help her out of this mess, it was Jesus.

She knelt beside her bed and closed her eyes.

Eight

G et that tire repaired?" Kate asked, pulling her softball gear from the back of Todd's truck.

"Yep. I must've run over a nail. Fixed now, though." He smiled at her. "Ready for the big game?" He gestured toward the baseball diamond, which was even now filling with members of Kate's church league.

She scanned the company of friendly faces, feeling the blood drain from her face. Despite Todd's coaching, she wasn't sure she'd ever be ready. Not to face other people's expectations. She already felt she was letting her team down by her very presence. It had been two weeks since she and Todd practiced, and her home-run hit was nothing more than a memory, fading almost to a dream. Had it really happened?

"It's just a practice," she said at last.

"Right," he agreed easily. "But they're going to play a practice game today. If they ask you, I think you'd make a mean first baseman."

She forced a laugh. "I don't want to be a mean anything. I just don't want to make a fool of myself."

"Kate," he said, stopping her words with a hand on her elbow. He turned her half around and stared deep into her eyes, making her stomach flutter.

He ran a tender finger down her jaw line. "I don't want to hear you talk like that. You won't make a fool of yourself. And even if you did, it's just a game."

"Yeah, they all say that," she mumbled. "Until we lose and it's my fault."

"Kate..." he warned.

Her lungs tightened. He didn't know. How could he? She smacked him lightly on the arm with her mitt and kept walking.

She heard the quick intake of his breath as he jogged to catch up with her. "What?" he asked softly. "Talk to me."

She slid a sharp glance at him. There was no use pretending she didn't understand what he meant. He had the disturbing capacity to be able to look right into her soul. She really didn't think she lived her life like an open book, but with Todd around she wasn't so sure.

She exhaled on a sigh. "I'm going to tell you a fairy tale."

He nodded for her to continue.

"Once upon a time, there was a little girl who really wanted to play kickball. And basketball. And baseball. It really didn't matter. She just wanted to fit in."

She slapped her mitt against her free hand, wincing at the sting of the leather. "But she didn't fit in. She was fat. And ugly. And though she tried her best, the children made fun of her and called her names."

"Mmph," said Todd, taking her hand and giving it a reassuring squeeze.

"And no matter how hard she tried or what she did to fit in, or even how well she played, she was always the last one picked."

She glanced at the baseball diamond, where the crowd was increasing. Her mind acknowledged that these weren't little children with mean tongues. These were God's people. People she'd worshiped with for years. She should feel welcome here. But the ugly sludge of fear only increased in her neck and shoulders.

"Or she was not picked at all," she whispered, finishing the tale.

Todd stopped her and turned her by the shoulders until she

was staring into his warm brown eyes. "And then she grew up into a beautiful swan, met Prince Charming, and lived happily ever after," he said, his voice low and tender.

Her stomach quivered with a thousand butterflies. She could almost believe it, coming from him.

Almost. But it was a fairy tale. She'd said so herself.

"No such luck." She turned and walked away from him, concentrating on keeping her pace slow and even. Taking deep breaths. Thinking about anything but the warmth in his eyes.

"You forgot something!" he called, and she turned back, steeling herself for his gaze.

He smiled and moved closer.

"Jesus loves you, Kate." He wrapped an arm affectionately around her shoulder and pointed her toward the baseball diamond. "And you have a game to play."

Dumb. He was the most lamebrained individual who'd ever walked the planet. More and more he was beginning to doubt his ability to minister to others. He couldn't even help the woman he loved.

Jesus loves you—and I love you, too. Inadequate. Inane.

Idiot! A clichéd phrase was not going to help her work through her problems. She needed a lot more than trite advice. But he was at a loss. All he knew was that the desire to step up to the plate for her was so intense he could barely control it. He *needed* to help her. Not because he was a pastor, but because he was a man. He was her friend and wanted to be more to her if she'd let him.

He found a seat in the dugout and sat back to watch. For a while, various members of the church team took turns at bat while others fielded. Kate had been talked into catching since she had a mask.

He found himself itching to go onto the field and redirect things. If they could see how well she played, they'd give her some much-needed encouragement, not to mention the position of first base. They couldn't tell anything about her skill with her kneeling behind home plate.

Deep down, he was terrified for her. It could happen again. Adults weren't completely impartial. They could damage an ego as much as any first-grade class could. And Kate could be hurt again.

He could relate. She wasn't the only one who'd been teased in school. His legs had been in braces to his waist until he was in third grade, and he was convinced that contributed to his lack of popularity in high school. He'd been a bookworm and hadn't gained his height and muscle until college.

He was still a bookworm. That was also due in part to the leg braces. He'd turned to reading when he couldn't play outside because of his physical limitations. But he didn't regret his past the way Kate did. He'd found God. Found something he excelled in. Found purpose and meaning for his life. It was enough.

Or at least it had been until Kate came along and ruffled things up.

Kate. She truly was the lovely swan of fairy tales. But she couldn't see it, and the knowledge ground on him like sandpaper. She looked in the mirror and saw a fat, ugly little girl.

He snorted aloud and shook his head, ostensibly at a grounder that the shortstop missed. She might have been a little overweight as a child, but he couldn't believe she hadn't always been pretty. Hadn't anyone ever told her that?

I will, he decided. Again, and again, and again, in a thousand ways, until she believed him.

"Hey, Todd!"

Todd snapped from his reverie to find Thomas waving his baseball cap.

"Come on down here and play with us. We could use the help."

Panic gripped his insides, but on the outside he smiled calmly and shrugged with nonchalance. "I only came to watch Kate. Thanks for asking, though."

"Well, if you're sure. We could use a man with your skill on the team."

"My skill?" he repeated lamely.

"You're a real superstar, to hear Kate tell it."

"Well, I wouldn't say that." He smothered a laugh. Heat flamed to his face.

A man Kate had identified as Pastor Alex blew a whistle, and the group assembled in front of the dugout.

"Okay, we've warmed up enough," he announced, waving his hands to settle the roar of chatter into a gentle swell. "Can we split into teams and play a short game?"

Kate shot an anxious glance at Todd. He felt his stomach knot. He knew she must be almost to the point of doubling over, though no one could see it. She stood calmly, her mitt tucked under her arm and her baseball hat at a cockeyed slant on her head. Her only concession to her feelings was the way she slowly rocked from one foot to the other, then back again.

She was nervous. And he was helpless. Why on earth was the pastor making them pick teams? Couldn't he just split them down the middle or something a bit more democratic?

"Ben," Pastor Alex said, gesturing to a man in his thirties, "you be a team captain. And Annette, you're the other."

The designated captains moved to the front of the group

when Kate cleared her throat and spoke up. "Don't we need to run through the basics so they can see what they're getting?"

"No," said Pastor Alex. "I'm sure they noticed who was who when we were warming up."

It wasn't fair! Todd wanted to shout. *Kate didn't get a chance!* She was catching, not able to show off her skills. If they could see her bat....

Kate looked Todd's way again, noting his grip on the bench and the strained look in his face. *He was worried about her!* Warmth flooded her chest, releasing the tension from her muscles.

A nicer man didn't exist; she was sure of it. He'd obviously gotten the gist of her little fairy tale, and now he was sitting in the dugout sweating on her behalf. She smiled at him, amazingly calm. Suddenly she didn't care what transpired on the baseball diamond. Knowing that Todd was there and that he cared was all that mattered.

Ben gestured for Annette to make the first pick. She chose a young college-age man who participated in numerous athletics. No surprise there.

Kate settled in for a long wait. She'd be Annette's last pick. Sexist, she knew, but true nonetheless. As a woman, Annette would feel sorry for her. More so than Ben, in any event. Yes, she'd lost weight over the years, but an athletic figure she did not cut. She wasn't kidding herself, never mind her teammates.

"I pick Kate Logan," Ben announced, and her eyes widened until she was certain they took up her entire face.

"Why?" she asked him as she moved to his side.

"Rumors," he whispered back as Annette made her choice. "Heard you're a real natural."

"What if I'm not?" She couldn't help playing devil's advocate, and she was more than a little disappointed that she'd been chosen because of her supposed abilities. Abilities that clearly had been exaggerated on her behalf.

Oh, what do you expect? she chided herself. Of course she'd be chosen based on her ability to play softball. That was what they were here for, after all. Maybe she was the one who needed to grow up.

"Mark Mason," Ben said, choosing a burly middle-aged man with a reputation for home runs in prior seasons.

"If you don't play well, then you don't," Ben continued. "We still enjoy the game. As the old adage goes, it's not whether you win or lose…"

"But how you play the game," Kate finished. "I know. Thanks, Ben."

"For what? Just do your best, Kate. That's all any of us can do."

It was a relief to hear it just the same. Especially from an athlete like Ben.

She glanced back at Todd, grinning at her from the dugout, and a thought occurred to her.

"Ben, should we invite Todd to play?" she suggested slyly, grinning and waving at Todd for effect.

"Nah. Pastor Alex already did. Said he didn't want to. Probably can't catch a ball or something."

"No," she immediately denied. "He's good. A real athlete. Why, he—" She cut herself short, realizing she hadn't actually seen him play.

But he had the build of a practiced athlete. And he had coached her, and she now felt confident enough to be here. He must not want to show her up on her first day, she decided. While it was magnanimous of him, disappointment battled irritation in her chest. She'd much rather have him play with her than just coach her.

Her team moved onto the field, and she grabbed her catcher's mask. For better or for worse, she had a reputation to live up to.

"You were fantastic!" Todd said, taking her bat and mitt from her. Her face was streaked with dirt in the lines of a catcher's mask. "Didn't I tell you?"

"Yes," Kate agreed, sighing. "Can we talk about something else now?"

"What? You don't want to talk about that double you made? Or how you stole into third, sliding for all you were worth? Or how you made that fantastic out in the last inning? Or—"

"Actually, no," she said. "I'm tired, I'm testy, and every last muscle in my body is screaming."

Todd was wired. Of course, he hadn't played in the game. But still. His heart was racing with her success, and he couldn't understand her relative disinterest.

He took her hand, lacing their fingers. "I have a fairy tale to tell you."

"Yeah?" She chuckled. "I hope it's not a long story. I'm about to zone out on you."

"I'll make it quick," he promised. "Once upon a time, there was a little girl. Okay, so she was all grown up. But she'd once been an adorable little girl."

Kate pinned him with a stare.

"Well, she was," he continued, defending his choice of words. "She'd been hurt before, and she was afraid to take a chance, but she did it anyway. And she was a rip-roaring success, and stole bases, and—"

Kate cut him off with another sharp look.

He cleared his throat. "The end."

She laughed softly. "Very nice story, Todd. But it really isn't necessary, you know. Sometime out there today, waiting to be picked last, I realized that it really doesn't matter in the big scheme of things. You know what I mean?"

He melted into her gaze. What that woman could do with a look shouldn't be legal. "Yeah," he said, cringing inwardly at the husky sound of his voice. "I think I do."

"I have you, Thomas, and Elizabeth to thank for it. I wouldn't have figured it out if you guys hadn't forced me to do something uncomfortable."

He felt decidedly uncomfortable now. "I think that's how God works, too," he croaked. The lump in his throat was so large it was amazing he could breathe, much less talk. "Doesn't it feel great to know that you've been picked for a team—*the* team—and that you weren't picked last?"

In his mind, he offered up a prayer of thanksgiving that not only was he on God's team but Kate was there as well. In some ways, they already were a family. If he counted God's family, which he definitely did.

The thought left him with a smile.

Todd smiled all the way home.

"What's that ridiculous grin plastered on your face for, you big lug?" Tam asked affectionately, greeting him as he walked through the door.

"What smile?" he asked innocently, wiping all expression from his face.

"Nice try, big brother, but that won't fly with me. You're beaming from the inside out."

He let the smile straining on his lips return. "She was fantastic!"

"She?"

"Kate Logan. The woman I was telling you about. She played her first game today. Well, I mean, it was only a practice game, but still."

Tam curled onto the couch like a Persian kitten. "I've got plenty of time. Sit down and tell me about her."

He lifted an eyebrow, suspecting foul play, but Tam just smiled and patted the cushion next to her.

"She's so…" he began, kneeling before his sister and taking her hands in his. "And she's…" He opened his mouth to speak, then clamped it shut again.

Tam laughed and squeezed his hands. "That good, huh? Is that why you've been so mysterious lately? I miss our heart-to-hearts."

He slipped onto the couch next to her and threw his head back into the cushion, closing his eyes. "I'm sorry. I've been preoccupied lately."

"With Kate?"

Suddenly desire welled up in him to share Kate with his sister. "I'd like you to meet her."

"I'd be honored."

The gravity of her tone surprised him, and he slit one eye open in order to see her expression. She was perfectly straight faced, but gentle humor gleamed from her dark eyes.

"Seriously?"

"Of course I want to meet her. Any woman who can get my brother's nose out of a book and into the real world is someone worth meeting."

Todd felt his cheeks redden, which only heightened when Tam began to laugh. He felt the corners of his own lips tipping up unexpectedly. "She really is a special one, Tam."

"I have no doubt. I have a good feeling about this one."

"Me too, kiddo. Me too."

Nine

———◆◇◆———

"Todd! What a lovely surprise!"

Kate heard her mother's exclamation from the garage, where, clothed in her grubbiest sweats and wearing a bandanna around her forehead to keep her hair out of her face, Kate was attempting to refinish a vanity. It was an old piece— of junk, her mother would say. But when Kate had seen it at a garage sale, she knew she had to have it. She saw it as a work of art, a lovely Victorian structure with intricate scrolling on the drawers.

Okay, so it was painted an awful puce color. But it was hardwood. Somewhere deep down underneath the ugly veneer lay a soft, gentle vanity with a personality all its own. And on this Saturday morning Kate was determined to find that character. She'd been stripping and sanding for an hour and was pleased with her progress, slow that it was. As she suspected, she had seen glimpses of the beauty of the natural wood below the layers of paint.

"Kate, come greet your guest!" her mother called, amusement in her tone. She knew full well Kate hadn't even showered, much less applied makeup. What was the point, when she was doing grunge work?

The point was that a gorgeous man could just happen to stop by and want to see her. Her stomach quivered.

"Tell him I'll be out in half an hour," she said, attempting to wipe pink paint flecks from her chin with her sleeve.

"I'll do no such thing," said her mother, appearing at the door between the garage and the kitchen. "That would be the outside of rude."

"Mother," Kate hissed through clenched teeth. "I can't let him see me this way."

"Of course you can, dear," Elise said, waving her daughter off. "Now get your pretty little face out here and say hello to Todd."

Kate sighed. Sometimes living with a stubborn, overbearing mother had its drawbacks. She grimaced, dusted off her jeans, and headed for the kitchen, where she stopped to wash her hands.

"Todd," she said, entering the living room. He was seated at the couch, but he immediately rose to meet her.

"I thought we could…" His sentence dropped off as he surveyed her from head to toe. His gaze moved with excruciating leisure, and she felt an increase in the heat rising to her face with every second that passed. If he didn't hurry up and laugh at her, she might spontaneously combust.

"…but I can see you're right in the middle of something." He grinned and stood back on one heel, crossing his arms over his chest.

"Yes, as a matter of fact, I am." She tried to frown, but it wasn't easy with him smiling at her that way.

"Can I help?" he offered.

"But I thought you wanted to—What exactly was it you wanted?"

"It's a surprise. But we can make it another day."

A surprise? For me?

She couldn't help the way her heartbeat increased in anticipation. No way was she going to let him talk her into putting off a surprise.

"Can you give me fifteen minutes to shower and change?"

"Take your time," he said easily, resuming his seat on the couch. "I can wait."

~~~~~

"You still haven't said where we're going," she reminded him for the tenth time in as many minutes.

"You don't make things easy on a guy, do you?" he countered. "I told you it's a surprise."

"Don't I get even a little hint?"

"You don't need one. We're here."

Her eyes widened as they pulled into a long driveway. The grass was amazingly green for early spring, and the bushes were all well trimmed. There were even multicolored tulips lining the huge sign that announced they were entering Roseborough.

Panic stabbed her, and she clamped down on her emotions. "I see," she said, tossing a cold look to Todd.

"Yes, precisely. I thought you'd want to see the place for yourself. Or at least, I thought you ought to."

"And so you took it upon yourself to make sure I did? Who died and made you my keeper?" She knew she sounded harsh, but she couldn't help it. Anger coursed through her chest, and it was all she could do to keep a lid on it. She slouched back into the seat, crossing her arms over her chest.

You can't make me was written all over her face, Todd thought, never mind her posture. Like a little girl told to clean up her room when she wanted to go outside and play. Except it was much more serious than that.

Well, he'd known going into this crazy scheme that it wouldn't be a simple task to convince Kate that her mother was making the right decision. He hoped to put her at ease, make her fully enlightened about if not comfortable with Elise's decision. And the only way to do that was to tour the facility and talk to the residents.

He knew she would fight him every step of the way. She

was one stubborn woman. But she had her mother's best interests at heart. He'd play on that to get her to agree. He was doing this for Kate.

"Your mom's going to do this whether you want her to or not," he said gently. "She's her own person, Kate. I know it hurts, but you have to let her go."

Kate stared through the dashboard. He reached a hand out and laced her fingers through his, covering her trembling hand with his own. He could feel her pulse pounding rapidly against his thumb. Not knowing what else to do, he squeezed her hand. To his untold relief, she squeezed back.

"I know I'm being stubborn," she admitted softly. "But I'm worried. I just want her to be safe. And cared for."

"She will be."

He tilted her chin up with his fingers until their gazes were locked. "She will be," he said again.

"I know," she conceded, looking away. "And I'm glad you brought me here today. I knew I had to visit Roseborough, but I've been avoiding it."

"You're in for a treat. What do you want to do first? Meet the caregivers? See an apartment? Have a round of golf?"

"I think I'd like to talk to some of the residents," she decided.

"Excellent se-lec-tion, mademoiselle," he said in his best French accent. He exited the truck and came around for her. "This way, please."

Kate laughed and jumped out of the cab. He always managed to make her laugh when she was feeling grouchy or depressed. "And who, if I might be so bold to ask, will be my tour guide?"

"*C'est moi!*" he said with a mock bow.

"Oh, good," she replied, looping her hand through his arm. She could feel the strength of his muscles under the thin broadcloth of his shirt. "Long-winded tour guides are my favorite."

He protested with a grunt and led her into the complex. The security guard at the front station appeared to know him, waving them right through the gate.

Kate filed this information away. It was soon followed by other tidbits…everyone seemed to know him, if the smiling faces and friendly waves were anything to go by. He appeared to be a special favorite of some of the older ladies, who flirted voraciously with the young man.

"Todd," she said, pulling him into a quiet alcove just outside the main building. "Is there something you need to tell me?"

The color on his cheeks heightened. For once, much to Kate's amusement and satisfaction, the man who always knew exactly what to say and do was at a loss for words.

"I, uh…" he began, then stopped. "I mean, I…"

"Uh-huh," she agreed smugly, trying not to smile at his discomfort.

"No, really, I…"

"Neglected to mention you work here?" she asked, finishing his thought.

He blew out a breath, looking both relieved and embarrassed. "It was on my résumé."

Everything came together in a second's time. She knew she'd heard of Roseborough before her mother dropped her bombshell—now she knew why. "No wonder you were on my mother's side!"

"I wasn't—"

"Well, you were encouraging her. And don't you dare try to deny it!"

"Guilty as charged," he said, flushing again. "I admit it.

And, of course, I should have told you. Only it didn't seem right at the time—when you were arguing with your mother, I mean. I realized you didn't remember where I worked, but I couldn't figure out how to phrase it delicately. Then afterward, I could never find the right time. It isn't exactly the type of information you can drop into casual conversation."

"So you devised this scheme to come clean with me?" Her heart welled in her chest.

"Yes, but that was only part of the reason. I wanted you to see Roseborough anyway. For your mother's sake." His jaw tightened.

"Apology accepted," she said with an airy gesture. "What's done is done. Forgiven and forgotten."

His shoulders dropped as he let out a breath.

She smiled. "Now, why don't you introduce me to one of these fine ladies making such a fuss over you and let me get down to business."

Roseborough wasn't nearly as bad as Kate had anticipated. In fact, it wasn't bad at all. It was clean, green, and friendly, full of caring people and a variety of activities.

She had to admit it—her mother would love it here. She could live alone but not be lonely. There were dozens of qualified people to care for her if she required help, but even more important, there were plenty of opportunities to make friends.

Her mother had been lonely since Dad died. Kate always assumed it was her mother's MS acting up, but now she saw beyond the disease and into her mother's heart.

Sometimes, Kate realized belatedly, family wasn't enough. Mom wanted—no, needed—to live her own life.

And this was the place to do it. Mom's choice. Kate felt the confirmation deep in her heart. This could be Elise Logan's new home.

And in just a few weeks, it would be.

"So?" Todd queried gently. "Did I tell it like it is? What do you think?"

She forced a smile, though her heart was still swimming with emotion. "I think," she said slowly, "that at least half of the ladies in this facility have a crush on you."

"Only half?" He looked mortally offended, his lips turned down in a frown.

She sighed audibly. "I guess I owe you a thank-you."

He grunted a short dismissal.

"I do," she insisted. "For making this easier on me. You more than anyone know how I've been struggling. And as always, you knew exactly what to do to help me out."

He frowned. "I don't always know—"

She waved him off. "Go ahead. Say you told me so. I know my mother will take great pleasure in saying the same thing as soon as we get back to the house. She was in with you on this, wasn't she?"

"Actually, no." He shook his head, denying the accusation. His eyes danced as their gazes locked. "It was all my idea. If it blew up in my face, I didn't want her to be involved."

"You mean if *I* blew up in your face."

"Why, Kate!" he exclaimed, throwing his arms up in the air as if to ward off a blow. "I would never think such things about you!"

She laughed. "Sure you wouldn't."

"However, I'm sure your mom will be relieved to hear you approve of Roseborough."

"Well, I don't know about that, but I'm sure she'll have something to say to me."

They reached the truck, and Kate waited for Todd to unlock her door.

He didn't. Instead, he moved to the driver's side and unlocked his own door.

She supposed she should be annoyed, but she was actually glad. The edge of perfection was wearing off of the man. Finally! Now maybe her heart could rest in peace.

But Todd didn't lean over and unlock her door from the inside, either. Instead, he reached behind the seat and withdrew the red plaid blanket they'd used when they changed the flat tire.

Grinning like a Cheshire cat, he stepped out of the truck and tossed the blanket to her.

"What's this? Another flat tire?"

"Well," he said, shrugging, "you wouldn't let me picnic with you last time, remember? You said you were already full of pizza as I recall."

She laughed and nodded.

"This time I made sure you were good and hungry before I asked. That way you can't turn me down."

"Hungry enough to eat a blanket?" she teased, waving the article in question.

"Actually, this is more what I had in mind."

With great flourish, he reached into the back of the pickup and brandished a large wicker picnic basket, removing it from where it had been hidden beneath another woolen blanket. *"Voilà, mademoiselle!* Lunch is served."

"Oooh. I like it. I like it!"

She did like it. She'd never been treated like this, most especially not by a man. And Todd made her feel...special. Attractive.

Loved.

The dawning came on her slowly as she walked with him to a large maple tree and watched him spread the blanket under it. He was everything a woman could want in a man and then some. He was sensitive and caring, yet strong and masculine. He lent a unique male perspective to her ideas, the two of them together creating something better than either could make apart.

She'd eaten with him, worked with him, ministered with him. And little by little, she'd given her heart to him. She tried to breathe normally, but the air hitched somewhere between her lungs and her throat. How could she have let that happen?

Todd dug into the basket and presented several fast-food submarine sandwiches with a flourish. "What?" he asked when he saw her face.

She shook her head and tried to smile. It wasn't *his* problem. And he'd obviously gone to a lot of trouble to please her.

"Who else have you invited?" she asked gaily. "There's enough food here to feed all the people in a Third-World country."

"I'm hungry," he said defensively. "And I assumed you would be, too. Now that I've solved all your problems for you, I mean." He handed her a can of Coke and popped the top on one for himself.

"Mmm. Humble, too." She watched him stretch out on the blanket, his broad, muscular chest close enough to touch. His chiseled jawbone was dusted with a five o'clock shadow. His warm brown eyes smiled up at her. So did his lips.

Those thin, masculine, excessively kissable lips.

She riveted her gaze to her Coke, willing herself not to look at him—especially his lips. More than anything, she wanted to kiss him. The force was so potent she wasn't sure she could resist.

Hah! What a joke. *She* wanted to kiss *him*. What was she

thinking? Her problems weren't solved. They were only beginning. And they appeared to be spontaneously multiplying with each second that passed.

"Kate." She was going distant on him again. It happened a lot, especially when they were alone together. Wanting to reassure her, he reached for her hand, gently uncurling it from the pop can.

At first she refused to meet his gaze. She looked at his shoulder, at the soda he'd set aside. Anywhere but at him. And when she did finally look at him, what he saw in her gaze hit him like a javelin through the chest.

Fear.

He was scaring her. The knowledge felt like hot lead in his veins. Was he moving too fast? Could she see how much he wanted to take her in his arms every time they were together? Could she hear how his heart pounded in his chest when she smiled at him? But no. He was certain he hadn't given himself away. He was determined to keep his feelings to himself until he was sure they were the right feelings, that she shared this incredible feeling with him.

If God didn't place this agonizing longing in his heart, this vibrant emotion that made him simultaneously feel both the happiest man in the world and the most miserable, then he didn't know who could be responsible.

And Kate was an incredible gift to a man who formerly believed God didn't want him to marry. He was a stubborn, hard-hearted fool. But God was bigger than that, willing to overlook his idiocy and give him his heart's desire, fulfilling a hunger he hadn't even known he had.

But Kate wasn't ready. And until she was ready, he would wait. He had no right to kiss her, not until he knew—and she knew—she was his for a lifetime.

Time. He smiled. That's all that was missing from this equation. He would give her more time to see that he was right for her, just as she was for him.

"Kate," he said softly.

"Hmm?" She tilted her head toward him.

"Would you come to church with my sister and me on Sunday? Tam is anxious to meet you."

"She is?" Surprise was evident in her voice.

"And I'm anxious for you to meet her, as well. She could use a friend like you."

"I'd be honored."

He broke into laughter. "She said that, too."

"Well, good then, you see? We'll get along famously."

"I know you will."

"Sunday, then." She lapsed into an awkward silence, and Todd rolled to a sitting position.

"What's wrong?" he asked quietly, stroking her face with the back of his fingers.

"I was just thinking," she answered, smiling softly. "I still have one major problem here."

"Yeah? What's that?" He had only one problem on his mind, and he was determined to conquer it. Sooner rather than later, he hoped.

"Mom may have found herself a great place to live, but I'm still homeless!"

Ten

I visited Roseborough today," Kate said casually, sitting down across the table from her mother.

The look of shock that crossed Elise Logan's face was well worth whatever discomfort Kate had originally felt when Todd proposed the idea.

"You did what?"

"It was Todd's idea, actually, and something I should have done much sooner. I'm sorry, Mother, that I didn't trust your judgment. Roseborough is a lovely facility, and I'm sure you'll enjoy living there."

"Who are you, and what did you do with my daughter?" Elise teased.

Kate laughed. "I'm sorry I've been so cross. You have the right to live your own life. I hadn't realized I was chaining you down here."

"That's not what it's about. You've given up your independence for me, and I let you do it. I needed you for a while after Dad died, and maybe you needed me in the same way. But just because I have MS doesn't mean I shouldn't have an active lifestyle, and I don't need to be a burden to you."

"You're not a burden."

"I know that's what you think, but I feel like a burden. Maybe I shouldn't have sprung the idea on you the way I did, but I'm not sorry we're going to move."

Kate sighed. "It's hard to think of living somewhere else."

"Have you found an apartment yet?"

"Todd and I spent a day looking. I found a nice place, but someone rented it right out from under me."

Elise made a sound of compassion and enveloped her daughter in a hug. "I know you know this, but everything will work out. God is in this. You're going to be stronger through this trial, as am I. We've just got to trust him to work out the details. And I'll always be there for you."

"I know that, Mom. I trust God, and I love you. I want the best for you. It's just hard sometimes."

"What is *with* you?" Tam stared at her brother from across the breakfast table Sunday morning, her dark eyebrows forming a line across her forehead. "If you droop any lower, your chin will be dripping with breakfast cereal." She paused and pointed to his bowl. "*Soggy* breakfast cereal," she continued, "because you've been staring at it instead of eating for the past five minutes. What gives?"

"Nothing," he growled, shoving his spoon into the bowl and stuffing a large bite of cereal into his mouth. She was right. It was soggy.

"Nothing as in your new job isn't working out?" Tam queried gently.

"No, of course not," he snapped, dropping his spoon back into the bowl, not caring that milk slopped onto the table. "There's nothing wrong with my job. It's perfect."

She raised an eyebrow but remained silent.

Todd pushed his bowl back and dabbed at the spilled milk with his napkin. "Sorry," he apologized gruffly. "I'm just surly this morning."

She gave him a reassuring smile. "So if your job isn't the problem, what is?"

He met her eyes, dark like his own. "I've managed to complicate my life a lot more than just my job. Although now that I think about it, I guess she does involve my job, too."

Tam's eyes lit with amusement and delight. "Aha! Kate! You're talking about Kate, aren't you?"

He narrowed his eyes on her. "I'm sure as shootin' not talking about my truck," he grumbled.

She whooped and exclaimed in delight. "Ha, ha! Kate strikes while the iron is hot!"

He frowned at her theatrical display. "What's that supposed to mean?"

She flounced around the table and threw her arms around his neck, cutting off his air.

"Easy, kiddo," he warned, pulling her arms away. "I need to breathe here."

"Now I really can't wait to meet her," she exclaimed. "I thought you might be falling in love with Kate, but now I know it's true."

Todd only snorted in response.

"What does Kate have to do with your job?"

He forced a smile and made a mock cringe with his shoulders as if he expected his sister to pelt him with something. "She's my—" he swallowed—"boss."

"What?" Tam screeched. "The pretty lady you taught to play softball is your boss?"

"Yes," he agreed miserably. "Stupid, huh?"

"Stupid? No—romantic is what I'd call it. Tell me more."

"What?"

"Details, silly. You obviously met her at work."

"Obviously."

"And you fell in love at first sight?"

He chuckled despite his ill humor. "Not exactly. I thought she was attractive, okay? But you don't fall in love with someone just because you're physically attracted to them."

135

Tam let out an extended sigh. "Don't start in with the brotherly lectures, please."

"Well, you shouldn't. And if I don't tell you, who's going to?"

"So she knocked you out with her looks and then won your eternal devotion with her wonderful personality."

Todd snatched the book she'd been reading at the table and flipped it over to discover the title. "What kind of books are you reading?" he demanded. "You sound like a hopeless romantic."

"All women are hopelessly romantic, Dunderhead," she said. "And you should remember that, especially with your beautiful Kate. You should send her flowers or something, you know?"

"She's not my Kate yet," he groused. "And I'd still like to know where you get those fancy notions in your head." He smiled to show he was teasing, but his mind had hooked onto her last statement and was twirling it around in his brain. "Do you really think I should send her flowers?"

"Of course, you idiot. And to clear up that other matter you mentioned, I do read an occasional romance. Not this particular morning, however."

"So I see," he agreed, tossing her copy of *Gray's Anatomy* onto the table with a thump. "I'm glad to see you spend some of your time studying."

Tam placed both her hands on his shoulders. "It's time to introduce your sister to the girl of your dreams."

This was a mistake. Kate knew it the moment she pulled into the unfamiliar parking lot. She was comfortable at her small home congregation, whereas this was a larger, community-type church. She turned off the ignition and watched several families enter the building.

She breathed deeply, trying to untie the knots in her stomach. In some ways she was thrilled that Todd had invited her to worship with him. It seemed like such an intimate gesture somehow, to go before the throne of God by Todd's side. Not to mention the fact that this was his home church and he would be introducing her to the important people in his life.

Then again, that's what worried her most. What would people think of Todd when he introduced Katie the Whale to them? More than anything, she didn't want the way she looked to reflect badly on him. She was nervous enough about meeting his sister without throwing an entire church full of people in. Which is why she'd spent an extra half hour on her makeup and hair this morning.

The sound of knuckles against glass nearly made her jump out of her skin. She looked to the left and found Todd peering in at her, a dark-haired woman with sparkling dark eyes right behind him.

Bolstering her courage, she stepped out of the car, smiling shyly, first at him and then at his sister.

Todd beamed back, the sunny grin that always made her heart flip-flop. "Kate, I'd like you to meet my sister, Tam."

"How do you do?" Kate smiled and extended her hand, which Tam ignored, instead wrapping her in an enthusiastic hug punctuated by a warm kiss on the cheek.

Todd chuckled. "Tam, this is Kate Logan, my boss and—" he paused and licked his lips—"friend."

"I've heard so much about you," Tam raved, linking her arm through Kate's and throwing her brother a smiling glance.

Kate chuckled. "Good things, I hope."

"Well, of course," Todd replied, sounding mortally offended. "What else is there?" He offered an arm to each woman and waggled his eyebrows. "I'm the luckiest man on the planet this morning, to be walking into church with the prettiest ladies around."

Kate felt her face go red. Does he really think that? His face shone with absolute sincerity and appreciation as he took in her face and outfit. She was beginning to believe he really felt that way.

She was once again taken by the ease with which Todd moved in his world, effortlessly greeting various members of the congregation, uplifting people with a word or a smile. And he introduced everyone he met to his "friend Kate."

She wasn't completely blind to the questioning glances thrown their way and couldn't believe Todd would be, either. People were clearly speculating on his new "friend," and Kate once again felt a blush of embarrassment creep up her cheeks. Did they think she wasn't good enough for him, that he deserved better? But everyone she met had shown her nothing but the greatest courtesy. She was the one prejudging, she realized. These were God's people. She offered up a quick prayer for forgiveness and for help to do better.

Todd led her straight up to the front of the church, stopping only to introduce her to Father Cliff, the pastor. He seemed delighted to meet her, only reaffirming to Kate that she was the one making mountains out of molehills.

"So far so good?" Todd whispered as they settled in their pew.

"Yes."

Tam stood and moved around Todd to sit on the opposite side of Kate. "I can sit by my brother any old time," she explained with a smile. "This way I can chat with you a little bit."

"Not once the service starts," Todd said with a pointed look at his sister.

Tam rolled her eyes. "He thinks I'm still seven."

He chuckled and folded down his kneeler. "I'm going to

pray for patience," he teased, kneeling and folding his hands in prayer.

Kate chatted easily with Tam for a few minutes, quieting once the organ music started. She knelt next to Todd, calming her heart before the service started.

Overall, she thought she did a magnificent job of keeping her mind on worship, though she had moments when her thoughts slipped to the man at her side, like when they shared a hymnbook and their shoulders brushed. But listening to his rich baritone quickly brought her back to the seat of worship, and it felt oh, so good to join him in song, jointly worshipping their Creator. In fact, she couldn't remember a time when she was more at peace than here by Todd's side.

"Well, does she pass?" Todd asked, pulling his truck onto the highway.

"Pass what?" Tam asked distractedly, folding her bulletin into a fan.

"The infamous sister rating-scale."

"Oh, you mean can you date her?"

"I mean a lot more than that."

His statement apparently got her attention because Tam dropped her makeshift fan in her lap and stared openmouthed at him.

He grinned widely at the bemused look on her face.

"I knew it was serious, but…"

"You don't expect me to disappoint all those people today who were wondering why Father Todd had a pretty lady on his arm, do you?"

"I didn't realize things had gone so far between the two of you."

"They haven't." He frowned, then shrugged.

"No wonder you were grouchy this morning. The lady in question doesn't share your feelings?" Tam sounded surprised.

"I don't know." He blew out a frustrated breath. "Sometimes I feel like we're getting close, and then she withdraws."

"What? You mean my handsome big brother is having problems attracting a woman?"

"Cut it out. It's not as simple as that."

She reached for his hand, squeezing it reassuringly. "I think she likes you more than you know. But I'll be praying for the both of you. If it helps any, I've invited her to attend my graduation ceremony."

Todd grinned widely. "You're a genius!"

"Well, I don't know about that, but I *am* graduating with honors."

"No, I mean because all our family will be there."

"I'm losing you."

"Don't you see? Kate will get to meet Great-Auntie Darcie and Great-Auntie Gwen."

"Oh, I do see. You're going to rope her into a wedding by using those old matchmakers to your advantage."

"Hey, a fellow's got to do what a fellow's got to do. Isn't that how the saying goes?"

"You're positive you want to bring Auntie Gwen into this?" Tam asked with a wicked smile.

"I can handle Auntie Gwen. You know how much she and Auntie Darcie want to fix me up."

She laughed. "Well, it looks like they're finally going to get their chance. Too bad you won't be a kicking, screaming sacrifice. That's always the best kind."

Todd swatted his sister from across the cab and laughed. "Yeah, you'd like to see that, wouldn't you, kiddo?"

"I've asked you to stop calling me that," she reminded him severely. "It just wouldn't be classy to call me kiddo when I'm dressed in my cap and gown."

"I'll try to restrain myself."

"See that you do."

"At least in public."

She crumpled her bulletin and tossed it at his head. "When they made the manual on big brothers, you were the model."

"Who else?"

"Does Kate know this?"

"No. And you aren't going to start making up stories, either. Not that she would believe them for a second."

"Then you've got nothing to worry about, do you?"

"Not a thing, kiddo." He ducked slightly as if avoiding the glare she tossed him. "Not a thing."

"Ten minutes and counting!" Kate stuck her head into the bridal dressing room and gave a friendly warning.

"Kate!" Lynda McMahon called, gesturing her inside and enveloping her in a warm hug. "Thank you for all you've done."

The cake was ready, the church decorated, the flowers delivered. This wedding had, Kate reflected gratefully, gone off without a hitch. Or at least, everything was set to go without a hitch. She never really relaxed until the rice was thrown and the couple were on their way to their honeymoon spot.

It always gave her a jolt of pleasure to see the culmination of her efforts in a man and woman being joined before God for life. Especially a couple as wonderful as Joe and Lynda.

"That's what you pay me for," she said, waving off Lynda's praise.

"I don't think so," the bride protested, loudly enough for her attendants to hear. "You went way beyond the call of duty for us, and you know it. I wouldn't be here today if it weren't for you."

Lynda darted a glance at the full-length mirror, and Kate followed the look.

"You look beautiful," she said sincerely. "Joe is going to fall right off the platform when he sees you in that dress."

Lynda's face blanched. "I hope not. My biggest nightmare has been tripping over my gown on the way up the aisle. I don't think it would be a whole lot better if he were the one to fall."

"You have a tea-length gown," Kate reminded her with a laugh, thinking of the sawdust floor in the chapel. Of course, it was now covered with a lovely red carpet, rolled out just for this occasion.

"Now you know why." She tittered nervously and reached out to take Kate's hands in hers.

Lynda's hand was quivering, and Kate gave it a reassuring squeeze. "Everything will be fine. I promise. Your Joe is waiting at the front of that aisle for you. Just focus on him, and let me take care of the rest."

Lynda's father came in the door, followed by a grinning, camera-laden Thomas. Kate slipped out, wanting to find Todd before the ceremony started in case there were any last-minute details he wanted to cover.

She found him just outside the groom's dressing room. He smiled as she approached.

"Everything okay on that end?" she asked with just a twinge of anxiety. Wedding days were always the most stressful for a wedding coordinator.

"Oh, yeah," he said easily. "I was just praying with Joe. That he wouldn't fall off the platform, mostly." His wide grin made her heart jump.

Kate swept a hand across her hair, mentally going over all the little details that would make the wedding and the reception that followed a success. "Not falling down during the ceremony appears to be the primary concern of both parties. You'd think they'd just learned to walk or something."

He reached out a hand and stroked his finger across her cheek, making her breath catch. His warm, dark gaze met hers, and she felt reassured somehow.

"You look as nervous as the bride," he teased, allowing his hand to run across her shoulder and down her back. Unable to resist the slight pressure he put on the small of her back, she stepped forward into his open arms, laying her head against the firm strength of his chest.

"Relax," he whispered, his breath warm on her ear. "Everything is going to be perfect."

She didn't see how she could relax with Todd holding her as he was, but surprisingly, she was able to close her eyes for a moment and refocus. He offered a quiet word of prayer for God's help and presence during the ceremony, and she listened to the thick, regular beat of his heart.

She'd had more than one daydream about what it would be like to hold him like this, but the reality far surpassed anything a dream could do. She was sheltered. Protected. Loved. And just for a moment, she let herself bask in those feelings.

"Hey, you two," Thomas called. Elizabeth was right behind him. As the bookkeeper, she didn't usually come to the weddings, but today was Todd's debut, and she'd insisted on being there.

Kate's eyes popped open, her peace shattered by the jolt of being caught in Todd's arms. What must her friends think? She stepped away from Todd and brushed a hand over her head, smoothing her hair with her palm. Her heart continued to hammer in her chest. She felt as if she'd been caught with her fingers in the cookie jar.

"Better stop your cuddling and get this show on the road," Elizabeth suggested with a knowing sparkle in her eye.

Kate crossed her arms and refused to meet Elizabeth's eyes.

Todd grinned at the two, clearly at ease. Which meant she was making a big deal out of nothing. Face flaming, she mumbled something about the time, hoping to make a clean break and get away from her friends. And from Todd.

"About that time," Todd said cheerfully. "Bring on the bride!" He looked directly at her and smiled.

Kate suddenly found it hard to swallow. She would not, could not, interpret that look.

Elizabeth nudged her in the ribs with her elbow. "I think he's got one right here," she whispered for Kate's ears only.

Kate looked at Todd then, and the warmth of his gaze filled her from top to bottom. Even her toes tingled. The gleam in his eye suggested he knew exactly what was transpiring between the two women. And the grin on his face suggested he didn't mind in the least.

The organ music started, and she excused herself, almost running in her haste to remove herself from the uncomfortable situation. Trying to figure out her relationship with Todd was difficult enough without Thomas and Elizabeth butting in.

By the time she double-checked the flowers and called the hotel where the reception would be held, she barely had time to slip into the back of the chapel before the bride walked down the aisle.

Every bride was beautiful, Kate had observed, with the happy flush of love on her face. And Lynda was certainly no exception. She looked lovely in an elegant Victorian-cut tea-length gown with a high collar and loads of lace on the bodice and sleeves. It was enough to take Kate's breath away.

For the first time since she'd opened her doors for business two years ago, she allowed herself the luxury of wondering what it would feel like to be the one elegantly gliding down the aisle as Lynda was now, every eye in the church upon her.

Always the bridesmaid, never the bride, that was Kate Logan. The cliché summed up her life in a neat little package. But today, for once, the thought didn't make her gloomy.

Kate followed Lynda's progress up the aisle, especially enjoying the pure, unadulterated look of joy on Joe's face as Lynda approached. The bride and groom locked eyes as they locked hands, then turned to the center to face the chaplain.

Kate's gaze moved to Todd. The center space had been empty moments earlier, but now it was filled and flowing with his large frame and strong presence. He was magnificent in his vestments, most especially the beautiful, multicolored woven tapestry on the stole hanging around his neck. An open Bible rested in his palms.

Over the past weeks she'd grown to know him so well that she'd wondered how she'd react to seeing him in the front of the church, decked out in his vestments. It was a funny feeling, knowing the man underneath the cloth. But he was definitely the right man for the job. A better pastor she couldn't imagine.

She was a little intimidated by the intimate glow in his gaze as their eyes met and held, but it didn't feel wrong. Just different. She knew without saying that the smile lighting his face was for her. But she didn't deserve it.

Standing up on the platform, very much God's man and obviously enjoying every second of it, the gulf between them seemed impossible to bridge.

Except by God's grace.

Todd lifted the Bible in his hand and nodded his head toward the bride and groom. But when he began to speak, his eyes were locked on hers, as if his words were for her alone and not for the two before him.

"Dearly beloved in the Lord." He paused, letting his words sink in.

Kate's breath caught and held.

"We are gathered together here in the sight of God, and in the face of this company, to join together this man and this woman...."

His voice faded as she struggled to comprehend what he was so obviously trying to communicate to her. He wasn't just reciting the words of the prayer book. He was opening his heart to her. She could see it in his eyes.

The rich timbre of his voice echoed in her mind. *Dearly beloved in the Lord.*

Joy washed over her confusion, leaving behind it a rare sense of peace. She'd not felt this way in a long time, since she was a small child. The wonder, the trust, set in concrete like building blocks at the bottom of her heart.

She leaned back in the pew, enjoying the warm wash of the emotions flowing through her. She could enjoy this wedding, not keep herself distant as she'd done in the past. She was always glad in her heart for the bride and groom, but today she could be glad just for herself.

Todd had cut through it all with his words, sorted out her flaring emotions. She wasn't afraid of this feeling anymore. How could she be, with the love of a Savior surrounding her and the comforting echo of Todd's voice still fresh in her mind, stirring little beads of pleasure in her heart?

To join together this man and this woman...

Eleven

Todd shifted in his seat and took another sweeping look around the auditorium. *Where is she?*

Kate had promised Tam she'd attend the ceremony, but there were only ten minutes until the opening, and he hadn't yet seen her.

"You're certainly antsy today," commented Auntie Darcie, adjusting Todd's clerical collar as if he were a seven-year-old boy. Auntie Gwen promptly dusted his shoulder, adding to his feeling of helplessness.

"I'm looking for someone," he admitted, his eyes still searching the gigantic room. There were people everywhere. His glance might pass right over her, and he'd never know it, except that he felt somewhere deep in his heart that he'd be able to pick her out of a crowd.

"Oh? A woman?" Auntie Gwen asked, scanning the room without even knowing whom she was looking for.

Or even, reflected Todd with an inner grin, *if she were a she.* He hadn't yet answered. The grin in his heart found his face.

"Oh, it is a woman," declared Auntie Gwen, patting Todd on the back as if he were choking. He straightened, trying to maintain his balance. It didn't matter that he was a full foot taller than these two ladies—they ruled the roost.

"What's her name, sweetheart?" Auntie Darcie asked, joining in the search.

"I hardly think knowing her name will help you find her in this crowd," he pointed out, shaking his head. "They aren't wearing name tags."

"Don't get smart with me, young man," she retorted playfully.

"Yes, ma'am. Her name is Kate."

"That's better. Now, what does she look like?"

Two pairs of eyes pinned him down. He swallowed hard. "Well, she's…and she's got…and …" His mind went blank.

"Todd, dear, you're going to have to get a little more specific if you expect us to help you," said Auntie Gwen. "Now, let's see. How tall is she? What color hair does she have? Oh—and her eyes?"

"Um, she tucks perfectly under my shoulder," he said, lifting one arm. "She has brown hair, the color of a ripe chestnut. And huge amber eyes." He smiled without meaning to.

"I think I see," said Auntie Gwen.

"Where?" asked Auntie Darcie, lifting her spectacles. "I don't see anything."

"Oh, Darcie, you silly bat, I meant about our nephew here. He's in love."

"Oh?" Auntie Darcie perched her spectacles on her nose and peered up into Todd's face. He smiled and tried not to pull away as she moved forward, examining him in microscopic detail.

"Why haven't you brought her to meet us?" Auntie Gwen demanded.

"That's why I brought her today, Auntie," Todd assured her.

"Well, you didn't do a very thorough job of bringing, if you ask me," she retorted.

"Actually, Tam invited her," he explained. But maybe his great-aunt was right. He should have offered to drive Kate, even if he had numerous relatives to sort out logistically. He made a mental note to apologize to Kate when he saw her today. If he saw her today.

The band started up with the traditional graduation tunes, and Todd was forced to take his seat, surrounded by his affectionate great-aunts and a horde of other relatives.

"Where did you meet her, dear?" Auntie Gwen whispered loudly.

"I work for her," he explained. "She's a wedding consultant who owns a small chapel. I conduct the weddings."

"Oh, how lovely," she said, patting his arm. "Don't recall when I've heard you talk so animatedly about a woman."

"Probably because I never have. I didn't do much dating during seminary, and afterward I was too busy with my work."

"If the stubborn, mule-headed man won't come to the woman, then we'll bring the woman to the stubborn, mule-headed man."

"I'm not sure that's exactly how the saying goes, Auntie," Todd said, laughing.

"Well, it should. It's about time you got interested in settling down. Young people these days, why, all they think about is work, work, work. Whatever happened to the good, old-fashioned notion of raising a family, I ask you?"

"Auntie Gwen," Todd said, his voice a warning. "Please don't start throwing babies into this equation with Kate just yet. We haven't exactly come to the point of discussing children."

"Well, why not?" intruded Auntie Darcie. "You've got to broach the subject one of these days."

Todd felt his neck go red. "Yes, Auntie, but not today. Promise me now, both of you. No babies."

They eyed him speculatively, and he recalled the blithe comment Tam had made about handling his great-aunts. He hadn't thought it would be a problem. Now, he thought, if he could find Kate before his aunts caught sight of her, he'd whisk her off without a word to them. He'd wanted her to meet his family, even with all their quirks, but he wasn't sure he was ready to explain why everyone had them settled with 3.2 kids and a dog and a picket fence before they'd even spoken of marriage.

He was a bundle of really dumb ideas where Kate was concerned. If only he'd learn to think things out to their conclusion before rushing into them, he'd be in better shape. Then again, he really hadn't been the one to initiate this hovering disaster. Tam had done the honors. She must have had something in mind, and it wasn't like her to be devious. Or maybe Tam just wanted Kate to see her graduate.

"I guess we're just going to have to watch the ceremony without Kate," said Auntie Gwen, sounding genuinely disappointed. "The graduates are starting to come in."

"Maybe we'll find her afterward," said Todd, his voice conciliating. *Or not.* He didn't know which was the better scenario.

Flush-faced, Kate tiptoed through the back of the auditorium. She should have known she'd need extra time to drive into downtown Denver. No matter how many times she went into the heart of the city, she got hopelessly and completely lost. The streets were all one-way and cockeyed.

She'd wanted to arrive at Tam's graduation exercises early to spend a few minutes with Todd, but instead the graduates were already receiving their final address. At least she hadn't missed seeing Tam receive her diploma.

She slid into a seat near the rear. It had taken her only moments to locate Todd, which surprised her since there were hundreds of people in the auditorium. She almost felt as if there were a string connecting their hearts to one another, pulling them together. But that was ridiculous.

She picked a spot where she had a clear view of him and of Tam. She'd intended to sit with him, but the only seat available was on the other side of a cheerful-looking gray-haired lady who had her arm around Todd and was playing with the hair at the back of his neck.

It made her smile to think of how he must be feeling, such a manly man being treated like a boy. It was a wonder he wasn't squirming all over his seat. What one wouldn't do for relatives. She wondered if the woman was a grandmother or an aunt.

She wouldn't intrude on a family moment for the world and decided right there and then she would slip out before Todd could see her. She would find a time to congratulate Tam later on. She'd want this time to be with family, as would Todd.

That theory flew out the window as Todd suddenly turned and looked straight at her. His eyes widened, then he smiled when she sent a tiny wave his direction. He gestured to the seat next to the old woman, but she shook her head, smiling so he would know it wasn't that she didn't want to sit with him. This wasn't the time or place. He pleaded with his eyes, but she continued to shake her head. Finally, he gave up and turned back around in his seat, whispering something to the two old ladies on either side of him.

They both chuckled, and Kate tensed, knowing they were talking about her. It wasn't like Todd to talk behind her back. Suddenly she didn't feel like being there at all. But for Tam, she would have fled the room in an instant.

Todd didn't turn around again, and soon Kate was caught up in the graduation ceremony. She cheered as loudly as the large group of extended family with Todd as Tam walked across the stage to receive her diploma with honors.

What a talented family. Todd and Tam's parents would be so proud if they were still alive. Kate certainly was proud to know them both. Caught up in the emotion of the moment, she completely forgot to make an early exit.

"She looked beautiful up there, now, didn't she?" said a crackly voice to one side of her.

"Oh, yes," Kate agreed, not even realizing the person was probably speaking of someone else. "She's so lovely."

"So are you, dear," the old voice said.

The jolt of her words nearly knocked Kate down. She whirled to see the owner of the voice and found herself staring down into the friendly blue gray eyes of one of the women who'd been sitting next to Todd.

"Why don't you join us, dear?" the lady asked kindly, linking her arm with Kate's before she had the opportunity to answer. "I'm sure Tam will want to see you."

"Oh, I don't want to intrude on a family gathering."

"Who's intruding?" said a strong baritone from just behind her right ear. Todd put his arm over her shoulder. "Tam and I both want you to be here," he said for her ears only.

Her heart warmed, and any thoughts of leaving fled. With a single sentence, Todd had turned her from an outcast to a wanted family friend.

Or had Todd done that? She pondered the thought. She was the one who had stamped herself an outcast. Could she not have gone up to a good friend and asked about the vacant chair, which she now realized his family had saved for her?

She had been putting herself down for so long that it was difficult to stop the process and realize that Todd and Tam really did know her and like her the way she was. Just as God knew and accepted her.

How much she had to learn. She sent up a quick prayer that she'd be able to salvage the rest of the day for herself, Tam, Todd, and their family. They deserved no less.

She received an open welcome from all his relatives.

Moments later, Tam joined them, whooping in delight and waving her hard-earned diploma in the air. Kate stood aside as Tam was accosted with kisses and hugs from children and oldsters alike. Todd was in the center of it all, laughing and squeezing the daylights out of his sister.

Kate laughed as a little boy of about two launched himself into Tam's arms and reached for her diploma.

"Oh, no you don't, Brady," she laughingly admonished him. "You have to go earn your own degree."

Suddenly Tam spotted Kate. Breaking through the circle of relatives, she threw her arms around Kate's neck. "I'm so glad you could be here. It means a lot to me—and to Todd."

Kate was unused to people wanting to hug her, but Todd's family was touchy in a good way. She reached out and hugged back.

"I wouldn't have missed it for the world, kiddo."

Tam laughed loudly.

"What?" Kate asked, perplexed.

"Kiddo. That's what Todd calls me. I made him promise he wouldn't say it in front of you. Ironic, huh?"

Todd placed his arm around Kate's waist. "Gotcha anyway, didn't I, kiddo? Er, I mean, graduate."

"The graduate. Now there's a title that befits my status," Tam said, sticking her chin in the air and posing as if she were a statue.

"Get over it," Todd said.

"Not yet, though," Kate said, patting Todd's chest. "This is her day. Let her enjoy it."

"Yeah, big brother." Tam linked her arm with Kate's on the side opposite Todd. "I think I'm going to like having another woman around."

~ ~ ~ ~ ~

Todd shifted his weight and pulled on his collar, which suddenly felt too tight. He'd been wearing clerical collars for years now without the least bit of trouble, but now he was wishing he'd bought one a couple sizes larger. He cleared his throat and rang the doorbell again. Either his collar was shrinking or his neck was swelling. If Kate's mom took much longer to answer the door, he was going to turn purple.

He felt a queasy mixture of relief and anxiety as he heard her slow, uneven steps just inside the door.

"Who is it?" she called without releasing the lock. He suspected she couldn't raise herself to look through the peephole in the door.

"It's Todd Jensen, Mrs. Logan," he called, surprised that his voice didn't squeak with the effort.

"Oh!" He heard the workings of the lock being opened, then the door swung wide. "Father Todd. What a lovely surprise."

Todd held his hands out to her, noticing their slight tremor as he gave them a gentle squeeze. He smiled down at her. "It's good to see you, Mrs. Logan. May I come in?"

"Well, certainly, dear," she said. "But you won't find Kate anywhere on the premises."

"Oh, I know that." He returned her easy smile. "I purposely came when I knew she was elsewhere."

Elise raised an eyebrow. "Mmm. The plot thickens. Please do come in. Make yourself comfortable."

Todd tucked Elise's arm under his and led her into the house. When he'd seen her settled on the pale blue sofa, he took a seat across from her on a Victorian high-backed chair in the same pale blue.

"Tell me what I can do for you. Something to do with Kate, no doubt. Is she giving you trouble already?"

He laughed. Her banter made him feel at ease. He would be glad to call this woman his mother. If Kate agreed to be his wife. And that was the razor-sharp point of the matter. He opened his mouth, but no sound came from his lips.

Elise laughed aloud. "Save your tongue-tied behavior for the young ladies, dear. No need to mince words with me. Whatever it is, it can't be worse than sitting there with it all caught up in your throat."

"Well, then, Mrs. Logan, I came here because I—er—" He cleared his throat and glanced at the floor. He sure was making a muddle of this. Renewing his resolve, he met Elise's clear blue eyes. "I want to marry your daughter."

He didn't know what to expect, but her calm reaction really threw him a curve ball.

"Yes," she said softly, pulling her glasses halfway down her face so she could peer over them. After a minute she nodded. "Yes. I thought that might be it."

"And?" he asked, half afraid of what her next words would be. She hadn't roared in anger or gone into hysterics. Good signs, he hoped. He'd always assumed when he was ready to marry, the in-laws, outlaws, and other appendages just came as part of the package.

And so they did. But for some reason he wanted Elise's blessing before the fact.

"And..." she said, picking up his thread of conversation, "I'm sitting here wondering why you're asking me about it instead of Kate. Don't you think you ought to discuss it with her? It seems the sort of subject she might have an opinion about."

"Yes, well, of course I should ask Kate, but I wanted to run it by you first." He wondered if he looked as flustered as he felt.

"Why?" She pulled her glasses down again and pierced him with a pointed look.

His face warmed under her scrutiny. He licked his lips and plunged in. "I know this sounds kind of old-fashioned. Corny, even. But I wanted your blessing on our marriage before I approached Kate."

Elise pushed her glasses back up her nose, clapped twice, and slapped both thighs with her palms. "Done. Now, go get my girl, and let's celebrate."

"Yes, well, that's the other reason I came," he admitted quietly, looking away.

"How's that?" Her voice was equally quiet, and he could sense her gaze upon him.

"I was sort of hoping you could tell me the best way to go about it. None of the scenes I envision in my head ever turn out right. I mean, sometimes it seems we've got a special, intimate relationship going between us, and then suddenly she backs off and closes herself up."

"She does that," Elise agreed, pinching her lips together.

"I know it's something I'm doing, but I'm tarred and feathered if I can figure out what it is that sets her off. And I can't afford for this to happen when I'm getting ready to pop the question. I'm relatively positive she feels the same way about me as I do her, Mrs. Logan."

Elise appeared deep in thought for a moment, her chest rising and falling with deep, even breaths. "Has she mentioned anything about her past?" she asked at last.

"A little. I know she hasn't dated much."

"She hasn't dated at all, Todd," she corrected. "Not since tenth grade."

He pulled in a surprised breath. Kate, not dating at all? He didn't understand. "But she's so beautiful and special."

"I'm glad you feel that way about her. Remember to tell her that every day of her life, for she doesn't believe it herself." Elise reached across the distance between them and took his hands in hers. "I believe you're just what she needs. The Lord knew whom to send."

Todd, too, believed he and Kate were destined to be together. But how could he, in all his weakness, provide strength to Kate when she needed it most? Every time he was with her he said or did the wrong thing.

"Maybe it would help if I knew what you had in mind," she suggested gently.

"Um, well, okay. Fancy dinner at a French restaurant. A dance or two. And then I was going to pop the question sometime around dessert." *If I don't lose my voice, or my nerve, or both,* he added silently.

"Sounds perfect so far."

"I was considering renting a tux and a limo. I really want her to know what she means to me."

Elise held her hands palm out in protest. "Now you're diving into murky water."

"Do you think so?"

"Wanting to please Kate is admirable, but you don't want to remind her of her senior prom, which I think a tux and limo might do."

"Bad experience at the prom?"

"No experience. She didn't go."

"I see," he said, mentally crossing a tux and limo off the list. "Plan B, then."

"Which is?"

He laughed and shrugged. "I don't have one." He bit his lower lip, considering the possibilities in his mind. "Flowers, do you think? Or is that too much, also?"

"Flowers are wonderful." Elise tapped a finger on her chin. "When is this spectacular dinner supposed to be taking place?"

"I haven't decided yet. Guess I'll have to wait until I ask Kate for the answer to that."

"I wouldn't do that if I were you," she suggested mildly.

"Do what?" he asked, confused.

"Ask her. You said yourself she has the most annoying tendency of closing off at the most inconvenient times. If I were you, I'd plan the dinner for as soon as possible and spring it on her at the last possible moment. She'll be too flustered to do anything but agree."

"You're a genius."

Elise bowed her head in acknowledgment. "Thank you for noticing, Son."

"I like the sound of that, Mom," he said, grinning widely, and ignoring the twinge of awkwardness at the word he'd once applied only to his dear mother.

"Yes, well, speaking of son—you and Kate do plan to give me a playpen full of grandchildren in the near future, don't you?" she asked.

Heat flared to his face. "I—er—well, I—"

"First time I've ever seen such a tongue-tied man of the cloth," she commented briskly. "Usually they're rattling off at the mouth, in and out of the pulpit."

He laughed despite himself. "I'll—er—do my best on the grandchildren issue, Mrs.—I mean, Mom."

She laughed in delight. "I'm sure you will."

"And I'll try not to bore you in the pulpit, either," he added with a wink, trying desperately to change the subject.

She eyed him frankly. "I think I'd like to hear you preach."

"Yes, ma'am, I'd like that, too. But I don't have the opportunity to preach very often. Except at weddings, I mean, and that's hardly the same thing." He rose and helped Elise to her feet, noticing her slight grimace of pain though she smiled and tried to hide it. "I guess that's it then, as far as my date with Kate is concerned."

"There is one thing you missed," she said, smiling up at him.

"And that would be—?"

"Your truck."

He stared at her blankly for a moment, then chuckled.

Of course. He couldn't very well pick Kate up in his truck for a nice date. But a limousine had been nixed, and his sister Tam drove a hatchback. He wondered what Elizabeth and Thomas drove, and, of equal importance, if they'd let him borrow one of their cars.

"I drive a Caddy," Elise said, breaking into his thoughts. "It's dusty pink, but if you can handle that, it's yours for the evening. It's a sleek-looking vehicle, even if I do say so myself. Just perfect for your date."

He nodded before giving it a second's thought. He couldn't drive Kate to dinner in his old, beat-up truck now, could he? She deserved at least a Cadillac, and in his eyes, a good deal more.

This night was, after all, the most important of both of their lives. He hoped so, anyway.

Twelve

———◦———

Kate slept better than she had in years, waking refreshed in time to make a big breakfast for herself and her mother. Not even the fact that her mother was hosting an open house later in the day, or that she was playing her first softball game of the season, could dull her good spirits.

She hummed as she stirred a skillet of scrambled eggs. In her mind, she tentatively explored her feelings for Todd. No doubt about it, God had sent him to her for a purpose. With his strong, quiet faith and gentle humor, he'd exposed her weakness to the light, made her face herself.

Funny, but instead of incapacitating her as she would have expected, she felt rejuvenated. A new person!

Love could do that to you.

Yes, it was true. At least she wasn't afraid to admit it to herself anymore. Somewhere in the past weeks Father Todd Jensen had slipped in and stolen her heart. Thick though her armor was, he'd found the chink that made her vulnerable. She suspected he had had God's help on that end—God already knew her greatest weaknesses. And her greatest need.

Dearly beloved in the Lord.

She took a deep, cleansing breath, and her humming turned to full-blown singing. To think that God might have better plans for her than she had for herself just made her feel like dancing.

"What a lovely sound," said her mother with a yawn, limping to the kitchen table. "I haven't heard singing around here since…well, at least since Dad passed on."

Kate rushed to give her mother a spontaneous hug of affection. "I know, Mother. It's been too long. But it's a beautiful day today—the kind of day to rejoice in the Lord, just for being alive!"

Elise laughed and patted Kate's arm. "What did Father Todd do to make you so happy?"

Warmth flooded through her chest and up into her face. Just his name sent her quivering. "What makes you think my mood has anything to do with Todd?"

"Oh, it has to do with Todd, all right," her mother confirmed with a wise nod. "Only a man can put that lovely shade of color on a young woman's countenance."

Kate set a plate of pancakes and eggs in front of her mother, then did a little pirouette in the middle of the kitchen floor. "Maybe I'm just—"

The doorbell interrupted her denial. Kate skipped out to the front door to find a delivery man holding a long florist's box.

"Ms. Logan?" he asked in a monotone.

She gave the delivery man a smile as big as her generous tip, then opened the box. Red roses. With a card tucked in. Were they for her? Maybe her still beautiful mother had a secret admirer. Her heart soared. Either way, it was a blessing.

She brought the flowers into the kitchen, inhaling their sweet fragrance as she went.

Elise's smile widened when she saw the bouquet. She pulled her glasses to the end of her nose and pinned Kate with a look. "You were saying?" she asked dryly.

Kate laughed. "I'm sure I must have been saying what a wonderful, handsome, godly man—oh, Mother, they *are* from

Todd!" She held the card with quivering fingers, staring down at the scratchy masculine writing.

"For our celebration dinner tonight," she read aloud. "All my love, Todd."

"What celebration dinner?" Elise picked up a fork and stabbed an egg.

"I have no idea." Kate set the bouquet on the table and curled onto a kitchen chair, rubbing the pulse points in her temples with her hands. "We have our first softball game today. Todd promised he would be there. Maybe he means after the game."

"Oh! A date, then."

"A date." She repeated the words as if they'd been spoken in a foreign language. "I can't believe this."

"Looks to me like you've got that fellow wrapped around your pinkie finger. Roses and everything. So, when's the wedding?"

Kate's head snapped up, her gaze locked on her mother's teasing one. "I'm not—we haven't…I can't believe this is happening to me."

"And why not? It's about time you decided to settle down. My goodness, Kate. You were a toddler by the time I was your age!"

"Yes, but don't you think it's odd that a gorgeous man like Todd would—"

"Katrina Marie Logan! Don't you dare say what I think you're going to say. Don't even think it!"

"What?" she protested. "I was only going to say that he—"

"Is too good for you?"

"Well," Kate hedged. "Yeah."

"Oh, that's fair."

"Huh?"

"You don't like it when other people judge you based on your looks, do you?"

"No, of course not. But that's not what's going on here."

"No? You don't think a man like Todd could love you. Why? Because he's good looking. Now tell me you aren't doing the very same thing you despise in other people."

Kate was silent. Her mother had a point. Maybe she was being shallow. Todd certainly felt something for her, or he wouldn't have sent her flowers.

Her mood soared. Maybe falling in love wasn't about being good enough. And if so...maybe it could happen to her. And maybe tonight was the beginning of something wonderful.

A pink Cadillac. He'd agreed to drive a pink Cadillac. Worse, he'd agreed to drive Kate in it. And it was her mother's car. What had he been thinking? He thumped down the stairs outside the office, taking the steps two at a time. Oh well. There was no use worrying over it now. He'd agreed, and he wasn't about to hurt his hopefully-future-mother-in-law's feelings by telling her he was too embarrassed to drive her car.

And it was a good sight nicer than his truck, even if it was pink. Never mind the fact that Elise's offer of her own vehicle was really a sign of trust, he thought. She had assured him that she welcomed him as the son she never had. His future had never shone so bright. Well, everything except his immediate future. He paused with his hand on the doorknob. Somehow he had to speak to Thomas and Elizabeth as if his insides weren't bouncing around like the balls in a bingo machine.

No sooner had he walked in the door than Elizabeth turned to him, narrowed her eyes, and placed her hands on her hips.

"What's up?" she asked. It was clearly not the usual polite rhetorical question.

He widened his eyes and tried to look innocent. "Not a thing."

"Kate just left for a client's house, so feel free to spill the beans."

He heard Thomas chortle from the opposite corner of the room. "What she means," he said, moving out of his corner and behind Elizabeth, placing his hands on her shoulders, "is that you are not leaving this room until you've disclosed every relevant detail of your private life. Isn't that right, Elizabeth?"

She hmmphed, then grinned widely and shrugged. "Something like that."

He grinned at both of them and then turned on his heels. "I'll admit to nothing."

"Oh, no, you don't," Thomas said, quickly scooting around Elizabeth and grabbing Todd's arm in a firm grip. "It wouldn't be Christian of you to leave me alone with a woman set on steam."

"Watch your tongue, or I'll steam you, Thomas Quinn," she retorted.

"I wasn't aware we brought personal business into the workplace," Todd said, trying his best to keep a straight face. He didn't really expect his ploy to work. He knew Elizabeth better than that. Besides, he was here to, as she put it, spill the beans anyway.

"I consider us friends," Elizabeth answered promptly. "You consider Todd your friend, don't you, Thomas?"

"Good." That was the opening he was looking for, since he needed their help. He only hoped he could stop from blurting out that he planned to ask Kate to marry him. When he first thought about it, he had every intention of telling them, but

165

then he realized it was insensitive to tell everyone in the whole world before asking the bride-to-be herself.

Besides, if she refused him, he'd have to come back to this very same office and try to work with these people. Of course, even if he didn't tell them now, they were bound to find out eventually. But he wouldn't think about that right now. He had a date to plan.

"It's like this," he began, rubbing his palms together in anticipation. "I'm planning to take Kate on a special date tonight."

"You sly devil, you!"

"Elizabeth!" Thomas hissed, his face paling to the color of his hair. "He's a pastor, for crying out loud."

Todd let her stutter and stammer for a full minute, quietly enjoying the situation.

"Well, he's a man, isn't he?" she blurted at last.

Todd burst into laughter. "I was wondering when someone would notice."

"Oh, I noticed," she immediately replied, then stopped as a blush rose to her cheeks. "I—I mean, I figure you've got feelings just like everyone else, even if you are a pastor. And you like Kate and everything."

Thomas linked his arm through Elizabeth's and led her to her desk chair. "I think you'd better sit down and shut up now before you make things any worse," he said affectionately.

"Thank you for your kindness," she muttered back, making a face at him.

"About that date," Todd reminded them, leaning his hip against Kate's neat oak desk.

"Oh! I understand—you want my help with it." Elizabeth branded Thomas with a smug grin.

"Er, uh, both of you, actually," Todd replied. "If I could."

Thomas shook his head. "I'm the last person on earth you should ask about the wild world of dating. Now, Elizabeth here, I'm happy to say, is a tried-and-true expert in the field."

"Every woman is an expert on dating," she informed them, her gaze daring either to disagree.

"And I sure need that expertise right now," Todd replied, which appeared to soothe her ruffled feathers. "But I do need you, too, Thomas. You're a close friend of Kate's, and you're a guy. I thought maybe you'd have some male observations that will help me do this all up right."

"Sounds special," Elizabeth said suspiciously.

Todd grinned. "Oh, it is. I love her, Elizabeth. I want to tell her so." *And ask her to be my wife.* He ran his tongue over his bottom lip and clamped his jaw shut.

"I know." For once Elizabeth wasn't coy or playing around. She gave him a gentle smile that surprised him both by its simplicity and its sincerity. "She deserves a man like you."

He chuckled. "I hope she agrees."

"I'm glad to hear it, Todd," Thomas inserted, extending his right hand to shake Todd's. "Ever since you started working here, Kate's changed. She's happy. Maybe for the first time in her life."

Todd's heart warmed. The thought that he could make Kate happy nearly overwhelmed him. He wanted to be the one making her happy every single day for the rest of her life. He only had to close his eyes to see her amber gaze full of warmth and laughter. Where she was, he wanted to be.

"I've got the date planned," he said at last. "What I'm having trouble with are some of the logistical details."

"Such as?" Elizabeth was all business.

"Well, I've got a reservation at Le Petit Chateau, for starters."

"Oh, Todd, Kate loves French food! She's going to be

ecstatic!" Elizabeth quivered with excitement.

"Well, now you've gone and ruined it for him," Thomas commented.

Elizabeth looked puzzled, and he shrugged. "The poor man can only hope for half the reaction from Kate that he just got from you."

"Oh, Thomas." She rolled her eyes and turned back to Todd.

"She mentioned once that French food was her favorite. Have you been to Le Petit? I've heard it's the best in the area." He rubbed his palms against his thighs, steadying himself with the rough, coarse feel of denim under his fingertips.

"Spending lots of money on a woman is a good thing, believe me," Elizabeth cooed, back to being coy. "With Le Petit Chateau, price is definitely no object."

"Well, actually, it is. But I'm splurging on this night," he admitted, grinning.

"You aren't taking her in that awful truck, are you?"

"Elizabeth!" Thomas hissed.

"Well, Todd knows what I mean, don't you? I don't mean awful awful; I just mean inappropriate for a date of this caliber."

"Good grief," Thomas mumbled and shuffled back to the safe haven of his picture table. "Women. What difference does it make what a man is driving?"

"Obviously a lot, Thomas, dear, which is why you're not married."

"Oh, you're one to talk, driving around in that little Subaru thing of yours."

"I'm not a guy, Thomas, in case you hadn't noticed." She let out a loud, exasperated breath, then turned back to Todd. "As I was saying—about your truck?"

"Kate's mom offered her Cadillac," Todd acknowledged

under his breath, shoving his hands in his jeans pockets.

"It's pink!" Thomas and Elizabeth chorused.

Todd smiled weakly. "She mentioned that. But a real man should be able to handle pink, shouldn't he, Elizabeth?"

"Of course he should. See, Thomas? A man who overlooks his own discomfort to win the heart of his lady. You should take lessons."

Todd shrugged. "It's nothing." And he sure wouldn't admit it if it were.

"When did you say you were going, again?" Elizabeth asked suddenly.

"Tonight. After the game."

"But there's a game."

"I think I said that."

"Yes, but—"

Todd stiffened, a brick forming in the pit of his stomach. "I blew it, didn't I? She'll be tired and probably sore to boot." He mentally kicked himself. "You don't think there's any chance she'll want to go out to dinner after the game?"

"Well, of course she'll go if she said she would. It's just that—"

"That's just the thing," he said, breaking in on her quick prattle. "I haven't exactly asked her yet."

Elizabeth leveled her gaze on him. "What exactly have you done, then?"

"Made a reservation?" he said.

"Todd, you are well and completely out of your mind. I didn't know Kate was a mind reader. What were you planning to do, show up at her door tonight and expect her to be dressed and ready to go by osmosis or something?"

"Well, no, but—"

"You've got to call her immediately." She whirled around

and marched over to Kate's desk, returning with the portable phone. "Do you need the number?"

He held up his hands in protest. "I know the number. But I'm going to see her in person in an hour. I was planning to ask her then. At the ball game."

"And the rational behind this would be—?"

"She can't say no," he answered firmly.

"Oh, yes, she can, and she probably will. I say you call her right this second." Again she extended the phone, waving it under his nose for emphasis. She sounded as if she were bossing a younger sibling around.

Todd straightened his spine. "I want to ask her in person."

"Okay, if you insist." She gave in with an easy smile. "But I hope you'll take my advice on this, at least, and ask her well before she starts to play ball. If something goes wrong at the game, you're going to be eating fancy blintzes and soaking up all that expensive French atmosphere alone."

"Are you kidding? Kate is going to be the star today. She's great at softball. You've seen her. I'm not worried about that aspect," he finished confidently.

"Are you willing to bet your fancy date on that? Even Babe Ruth had a bad day now and again, didn't he?"

He shrugged in concession. "You're right. I'll ask her before the game. There are too many variables for me to wait until later."

"See, Thomas?" she called over her shoulder. "He's sensible, too."

"Already knew that," Thomas muttered. "And he has the patience of a saint to put up with your noise."

"I expect Kate could use your help preparing on such short notice," Todd continued.

"Oh, I'd love to." Elizabeth squealed.

"You probably know about clothes and stuff."

"Probably," she agreed, grinning. "I recall to mind that Kate has a flow-y spring number that would be lovely."

He shook his head. "Don't talk to me about clothes, please. I draw my line at pink Cadillacs. I've spoken to Elise Logan, though, and I'm sure she'll be happy to help."

"I'll give her a call."

Todd nodded and moved to his own desk on the opposite side of Kate's. He shuffled through some papers, then turned to go. "Thanks for your help, Elizabeth." He waved toward the back corner. "You, too, Thomas."

Thomas chuckled and came forward to shake Todd's hand again. "I told you I wasn't going to be much use to you today."

"That's okay, Thomas. You can take pictures at our wedding."

Both men heard Elizabeth's sharp intake of breath and whirled toward her. Thomas was the first to act, pouncing forward and clamping his hand over Elizabeth's mouth, enhancing the impression that her eyes were bulging.

She said something underneath his hand and tried to squirm away, but Thomas held fast.

"No, Elizabeth, dear. Calm down. Deep breath in. Deep breath out."

Todd was certain he caught a "But" this time, and she squealed and prattled under Thomas's hand.

"It was a joke. Don't start sending out the invitations."

Just yet, Todd added in his mind. With God's good providence shining down on him, he hoped by tomorrow he'd be asking Elizabeth to do just that.

"We'll see you at the game," Thomas said, putting his arm

around Elizabeth and leading her away, his hand still firmly over her mouth. He shot Todd a knowing look and shook his head. "Women."

Todd grinned. Women, indeed. For all Thomas's blustering, Todd couldn't recall a time he wasn't by Elizabeth's side. Not only in work, but also socially, they appeared attached at the hip. They had a strong, enduring friendship. Perhaps that was what allowed their banter. No one's feelings got hurt, at least very often, and then apologies were quickly rendered and wounds repaired.

He hoped his own relationship with Kate would be so sustaining, to be able to tell each other the truth in love and to fill their home with laughter.

But he was getting ahead of himself again. First he had to ask her to marry him, and the time was growing near.

Thirteen

R eady for the game?" Todd scooped up the gear from the back of his pickup and gestured for Kate to walk with him. It was a nice, sunny day for a game, and he knew Kate was going to be great.

"Yes, actually, thanks to you. I'm nervous, but I'm not afraid."

His gaze met her clear, sparkling eyes. "I'm glad for that," he said, his voice unnaturally low and husky. "But I can't take all the credit."

She smiled gently, and he wished he had a free arm to put around her.

"No, I suppose you're right. I've got God to thank as well," she said softly. "But there is another issue I ought to address, don't you think? Something specifically concerning you?"

"Mmm? What?" His mind was already wandering to popping the question. Or, more accurately, popping the questions. He had to invite her to dinner before he could ask her to be his wife. He didn't know which proposal was making him more nervous, but he did know his knees were knocking under the cover of his black denim jeans.

"The roses," she said, chuckling. "How quickly we forget. I've never received such a lovely gift in all my life."

Her face was positively glowing with pleasure, and Todd's heart welled in his chest. He'd have to remember to thank his sister for her input in his pathetic attempt at romance.

He'd go buy another dozen after the game. Everything had to be perfect for tonight. Anything to please his Kate.

Aloud he said, "It was nothing."

"Not to me it wasn't," she insisted. "Thank you."

He smiled, unable to speak around the lump in his throat. She was so beautiful. Her chestnut hair shone in the morning sunlight, and her eyes sparkled with delight. She literally took his breath away.

"About tonight…" she prompted.

"Tonight," he repeated, wondering why he was finding it so difficult to speak.

"What I meant was, what *about* tonight? What's this about a celebration dinner?"

"Well, of course!" he exclaimed, regaining his speech, if not his mental faculties. "We'll want to celebrate, won't we?"

"What if we lose?" she asked, laughing at his enthusiasm.

"Not a chance." He took a deep breath to still his pounding heart. He wondered if Kate could hear it. "But even if you do, I still want to take you out to dinner."

Before she could accept his invitation, they were beckoned from the field.

"Todd! Kate! It's about time you two showed up," called Elizabeth, approaching them from the baseball diamond. Thomas was right behind her.

Elizabeth questioned Todd with her gaze, and he answered with a slight shake of his head. She let out an audible breath, and Todd shrugged. He was trying, for heaven's sake. What else could the woman expect of him?

"What's the matter? You thought I wouldn't show?" Kate teased, shaking her head at her friends.

"We've got a problem," Thomas said, leaning an elbow on Elizabeth's shoulder and receiving the glare he was clearly expecting in return. She swiped at him with her hand, but he jumped out of her way before she could land a blow.

"Cut it out, you two," Kate admonished as firmly as she

174

could while laughing. "Now tell us what's wrong."

"Ken Baker canceled out. We're short one guy." Elizabeth looked straight at Todd.

He could see what was coming before the words left her mouth. It would be easy enough for him to turn Elizabeth down, but Kate turned her gaze on him as well, and as soon as he saw her eyes, he knew he was a goner.

It figured that he'd put on a pair of jeans and a T-shirt this morning. He'd thought about wearing his clerical collar, which would have effectively disqualified him from playing.

But no. He was dressed like a man ready to play a game of softball. And that, it appeared, was exactly what he was going to be doing in just a matter of minutes.

"I really only came here to lend Kate moral support," he protested.

"But we need you to play," Thomas interrupted.

"Kate needs you," Elizabeth added in a low purr. "Don't you, Kate?"

Todd looked to Kate. She gave him an intense look and then shook her head at her friends. "If he doesn't want to play, then he doesn't. You can't force the man to do what he doesn't want to."

He didn't miss the way she'd distanced herself from him, talking about him in the third person as if he weren't even there, when moments ago they were talking animatedly. Intimately, even.

Please, God, don't let her withdraw from me. Not today.

He couldn't have her push him away today of all days. He still hadn't quite gotten the hang of her mood swings yet, the way she was so open with him one moment and so closed off the next. But whatever was going on in that pretty little head of hers, he had to put a stop to this withdrawing thing right now.

175

And he could think of only one sure way to do it.

"I didn't say I wouldn't play," he said, looking straight at Kate. "I only said I hadn't planned to play. If Kate wants me to help, I'll help."

Yeah, sure. Help them lose, most likely. In just a few short minutes Kate was going to get a good, hard look at the real Todd Jensen in all his glory. It figured that it had to be right before the most important dinner of his life. He knew the time was coming when he'd have to come out of the closet and admit he was a bookworm and not a jock. *But why, God, does it have to be today?*

The alternative was unthinkable. If he didn't offer his help, Kate would close off completely, and any thoughts of a romantic evening for two would be up in flames.

"First base?" Thomas asked, slapping him on the back.

"Um...I was thinking outfield. Right side."

"No way," Kate protested. "You need to be where the action is." She looped her arm through his and leaned into him so she could speak for his ears only. "You don't have to worry about outshining me or anything. I can take it."

Oh, sure. *She* could take it. He had no doubt about that. *She* could play softball.

He couldn't.

"Oh, I won't," he said, shifting his gear to one side so he could put an arm around her waist. "I promise." It was, he reflected, going to be an easy promise to keep. And the worst of it was, she hadn't agreed to accompany him to dinner. He was at the mercy of the game in more ways than one.

The four of them joined the team in the dugout, and the game was soon underway. Todd was given the shortstop position, which was Ken Baker's usual spot.

For over an hour he managed to look like he was contributing while letting those around him make the big plays. He found if he braced his feet, pulled his cap down low over his brow, and punched his mitt like the others, he looked like he was participating. Just so he didn't get in the way of the ball.

Kate was spectacular, as he knew she would be. She was first on the batting line-up and promptly hit a double. She stole third and slid into home to make their first score of the day.

Todd started to relax. His team was winning even with him out on the field pretending he knew what was going on. Shortstop wasn't half bad, he decided. He let the basemen field for him, and no one was the worse for wear. Another half hour and they'd be finished. Then the real fun would begin. Or at least he hoped so. He still wasn't completely certain of the outcome of the evening, of the plans he had laid. A lot hinged on Kate's reaction.

Whom was he kidding? Everything depended on her reaction. And with Kate, nothing was a certainty. Like a pendulum, she could just as easily swing one direction as another.

He was still musing on the possibilities, acting out his role in his mind, rehearsing what he would say, when the third baseman hollered his name. He looked up, wondering what the commotion was about.

The batter was pointing his bat right at him, Babe Ruth style. The pitch flew fast and straight. Todd heard the crack of the bat as the ball made contact, but he stood frozen as the big white ball flew with unbending accuracy straight for his head.

Kate couldn't help the grin that crossed her face when the batter cracked a shot directly at Todd. It was about time he was forced to play! She had expected him to be a more active shortstop, but he had yet to field a single ball. He'd swung and missed at his turn at bat. She could have told him he was swinging too soon, but then, he already knew that. He was obviously doing it on purpose.

She couldn't see where his hitting a home run would have hurt matters, but she supposed he was holding back on her account. Chivalry was nice, but at the same time, the game was at stake. And it wasn't like she'd go running and screaming off the playing field if he played well.

Anger sparked to life in the pit of her stomach. If he didn't play on her account and they lost, it would still be her fault. How did he think that could be considered "helping" her?

She watched as the ball sailed directly for him. He couldn't avoid this one. The ball was his and his alone to field. He should have his mitt up and cocked as he'd taught her, she thought belatedly.

Instead, he dropped to one knee, and the ball soared over his head and into the outfield.

The outfielder threw it back in, but not before the batter ran a double. It was a rough play, and Todd was to blame. But as soon as the play was completed, the team ran to his side to see if he was okay.

Kate wanted to scream. He couldn't have sprained an ankle, and she'd bet her next paycheck he didn't have a bad knee, either. What he had was an overactive Prince Charming gland that caused him to be chivalrous at the most inconvenient times.

Well, this time he'd crossed the line, and he was going to hear about it. She didn't need him bowing out of the game on her account. She threw her catcher's mask to the ground, followed by her mitt, creating a cloud of dust. She pushed through the crowd around Todd until she stood glaring over him, hands on hips, ignoring the murmurs of concern around her.

Todd stood and brushed off his jeans. "I'm okay, really," he said with an apologetic shrug in her direction. "Let's play ball."

Kate waited until the team began to return to their positions before she spoke. "I had better," she said, her lungs burning with barely restrained emotion, "see you batting, fielding, and sliding through the dirt in the next two innings."

His dark eyes blazed, but he didn't speak.

"Or else," she continued, trying to come up with a threat that would mean anything to Todd.

He gave her a cocky grin that didn't quite reach his eyes, as if daring her with her words. *Or else, what?* his gaze seemed to ask.

Her mind drew a blank. "Or else," she concluded lamely, the fire extinguished from her tone.

"I'll play ball the way you want," he said, his voice low and controlled, though his breath was coming in short gasps.

She'd obviously made him angry. Well, so be it. If he felt he couldn't play a stupid softball game because he might hurt her feelings, then he didn't know her very well. The thought struck her that before she'd met Todd, her feelings *would* have been hurt by such an action. He'd been the one to help her rise above those feelings, get beyond her fear, but he wasn't giving her a chance to prove it.

He wasn't finished. "If you promise you'll have dinner with me, no matter what happens. Deal?"

"Batter up, Kate!" Thomas yelled from the dugout. "We need our catcher!"

Kate met Todd stare for stare, noticing with some relief that the familiar twinkle of laughter was back in his gaze.

"Deal," she said finally, tugging the brow of her cap down over her eyes. "Now, let's play ball!"

It was immediately, painfully apparent, at least in Todd's

mind, that he'd been withholding the truth from Kate and her team. He made the effort he promised, with mixed results. Whatever he did, he didn't look in Kate's direction. Not when he fouled himself into oblivion before finally hitting a single, and not when he tangled with the baseman trying, unsuccessfully, to steal third as Kate had done.

He fielded a few balls with a measure of accuracy. The grounder he scooped up that beamed him in the head before dropping back into his mitt wasn't one of his finer moments. At least Kate's church won in spite of him.

Kate caught up with him moments after the game was over and the teams had come together. "That was absolutely the most incredibly amazing thing I have ever had the privilege to witness," she said, removing her cap and wiping her forehead with the side of her wrist, streaking her face with dirt.

He ran the pad of his thumb over her cheek, removing one particularly glaring smudge. "What was?"

"How…how did you teach me to play softball?"

"Why do you ask?" he queried, playing dumb.

"Why do I ask? Oh, maybe because my suspicions have been building all afternoon. At first I thought you were just trying to be nice to me, not show me up, you know?"

He nodded miserably, throwing their gear into the back of his pickup.

"Even when you ducked under that first ball, I thought you were doing it for me." She paused and gave him a full-tooth grin. "But when you beaned yourself with that grounder, I knew something funny was going on. Todd, you taught me to twist my wrist when I caught a grounder so the ball wouldn't roll up and hit me in the head."

"Guess I did, didn't I?"

"Speaking of which, how is your head? It must have hurt.

That ball was coming at a pretty good clip."

He chuckled and knocked on his skull with his closed fist. "Good as ever. The rocks in my head are good for something, you know."

"So you can't play softball," she said, so amazed she must have been withholding her final judgment until he told her the truth.

"Um…actually, no." He braced himself for the onslaught he was sure would follow.

"If that doesn't beat all," she said, laughing quietly.

"You're not mad?"

"No, of course not. I am curious, though. How did you teach me to do things you can't do yourself?"

"Head knowledge. Tam taught me," he admitted. "She really is an expert."

"I thought all little boys learned to play baseball."

He pierced her with his gaze, then looked away. "Yeah, well, not this little boy."

She waited in silence for the rest of his explanation.

He shrugged. "I had braces on my legs until third grade."

"I'm sorry," she whispered, taking his hand and lacing her fingers through his. "I didn't know."

He tried to smile, but it felt more like a grimace. "Of course you didn't. I couldn't play the games little boys played, so I learned to find my adventure in books. By the time my braces came off, I was already branded a bookworm, and you know what that does to a kid's reputation."

Kate nodded solemnly.

"I really never had the inclination to learn after that. I think I must have convinced myself that athletics weren't for me. I work out now, but that's only been the past few years. Guess I should have tried harder to brush up on my skills, huh?"

"You taught me," she reminded him.

"It was a stupid thing to do," he admitted. "Do you forgive me for not telling you the truth?"

"As long as you keep smiling at me like that, I'll forgive you anything."

"Are we still on for tonight?" He choked out the question fearfully.

Her face sobered, and her eyes shadowed just enough to cause Todd's heart to stop beating.

"Yes, of course," she said at last.

The breath he'd been holding came out in an audible huff. His smile was so wide he thought it might split his face, but he couldn't help it. As long as Kate was with him, he was happy.

"I promised, didn't I?" she teased. "I can't very well bow out now."

He felt like whooping, like proclaiming his love for Kate to the world, yelling it from the rooftops, even. The only thing that prevented him from doing so was that he thought he should probably tell Kate first.

He chuckled at his own joke.

"What's so funny?" she queried, looking at him suspiciously.

"Oh, nothing. Private joke. You wouldn't understand."

"I see," she said dryly, shaking her head.

"Six o'clock sharp," he said. "For dinner, I mean. I'll be waiting on your doorstep. Don't be late."

"I won't," she affirmed.

"And Kate," he continued, reaching out to smooth her hair away from her face.

She looked away, suddenly shy.

"Put on your prettiest dress."

"What?" she squeaked, looking at her watch. "You want me ready for a *nice* date in two hours?"

"Well, yeah. Sure." It would take him fifteen minutes to shower and another ten minutes to shrug into his suit. He figured a woman could only take twice as long. That left a good hour at least. What was she squawking about?

"You should have warned me days ago!" she admonished in a wail. "I've got to go get help. See you at six."

He watched, dumbfounded, as she literally ran back to the field, hollering at the top of her voice for Elizabeth as she went.

Women. Maybe Thomas was right. He'd never understand them if he lived to be a million years old. He shook his head and climbed into his truck.

He, at least, would be ready for dinner at six o'clock. His stomach was rumbling already.

Fourteen

T he doorbell rang, and Kate cringed.

"Oh, cut it out, silly," said Elizabeth, swatting her with a brush. "If you keep moving like that, I'm never going to be able to get your hair done before Todd gets here!"

"Sorry. I'm just nervous, I guess."

"Well, don't be. You're going to knock that man's socks off after I get done with you."

"Do you think so?" Kate peered into the mirror.

Elizabeth was, indeed, working wonders. Kate's straight hair had been ironed into loose curls that framed her face. She had protested when her friend insisted she buy fifty dollars' worth of new makeup and a bottle of expensive perfume, but now she could see the results were worth every penny.

The cool coppers and dark browns of her eye shadow gave her an elegant, yet understated, look. Elizabeth had framed her eyes with liner, making her large eyes the focal point of her face. It was very effective, and Kate was glad she'd asked for help.

"Maybe you missed your calling," she said as Elizabeth brushed light rouge across her cheeks.

"Ah, but didn't you know? On Saturday nights, I metamorphose from mild-mannered accountant to makeup artist extraordinaire."

Kate laughed. It certainly boosted her confidence a notch or two to see the woman gazing back at her in the mirror. She could scarcely believe it was her own reflection.

"Oh, stop gawking at yourself and come see what just arrived at the door for you," said Elise Logan from the doorway.

"You won't believe it unless you see it."

"Come on!" Elizabeth exclaimed, pulling on the sleeve of her terry-cloth bathrobe. "Let's go see what it is!"

Kate reluctantly followed her mother into the living room, half expecting to find Todd there. Elise, Kate was convinced, thrived on throwing her daughter into embarrassing situations just to see how well she would cope. But jaded as her thoughts were, she couldn't help the exclamation that left her mouth when she saw the enormous ceramic planter filled to the brim with red roses.

"The color of love!" her mother singsonged. "He's sending you a message, loud and clear!"

The flower arrangement dwarfed the coffee table, and Kate had to maneuver the vase around so that she could sit on the couch and enjoy the heady fragrance. She plucked the card from the arrangement and turned it over in her hand, shading the writing from curious onlookers.

Until tonight, it read. *All my love, Todd.*

"How perfect!" Elizabeth gushed, taking a huge whiff of the bouquet. "He is s-o-o-o-o-o romantic I can hardly stand it! And Kate, we bought you rose-scented perfume for tonight!"

That was no coincidence, Kate thought with a secretive smile. Somehow, she thought Todd might associate her with roses after this morning's delivery. Better that than Eau de Sweaty Softball, in any case.

Now it seemed perfect. Another one of those little details God worked out in the lives of his beloved.

"There's a corsage somewhere under all that foliage," said her mother with a smile. "A red rose, if I'm not mistaken."

"And you wearing emerald green," sighed Elizabeth. "Oh, what I wouldn't give to be a fly on the wall in that restaurant tonight. By the way, where's he taking you?"

"I don't know. I've never seen him so secretive. All he would say is formal dress." She rolled her eyes at the smug look Elise gave her. "Whatever you're thinking, Mom, just cut it out. He's taking me on a date. Let's not read grandchildren into the picture just yet."

"I wouldn't be so sure of that," Elizabeth piped up. "Grandchildren have often been the natural end product of dinners like these."

"Thanks a lot, girlfriend," Kate gibed, tossing her a friendly glare.

"Well, someone has to say it," countered her mother. "I'm glad you have friends like Elizabeth to show you the potential of certain...shall we say...opportunities?"

"Mother! You make it sound like I ought to walk into the restaurant, lasso Todd around the neck, hog-tie him, and drag him to the nearest altar."

"You're the wedding expert," Elise replied. "Do it your way."

"I'm going to be the most severely underdressed wedding expert at the restaurant tonight if I don't get back in there and get my dress on!"

Elizabeth glanced at the clock. "Fifteen minutes! Kate! We only have fifteen more minutes!" She blew like a hurricane back into the bedroom.

Still chuckling, Kate moved to follow her, but Elise stopped her with a hand on her arm.

"Just a moment, Kate, if you please?"

"I hate it when you use terminology like that," she grumbled, allowing her mother to draw her into the kitchen. "It always means bad news."

"Not bad news, exactly."

"Oh, no." Kate steeled herself, but nothing could prepare her for her mother's next words.

"I'm moving tomorrow."

Kate sucked in a breath. *"Tomorrow?* Why so soon? We don't even have an offer on the house yet."

"Actually, we do. I got a firm offer this afternoon. These folks are anxious to get into the house, and I assured them we'd seal the deal as quickly as possible."

"I see." A knot tightened in the pit of her stomach.

"And I need you to do me a favor."

"What is it?" she asked through clenched teeth. *Not now, Mom,* her heart cried out. *Don't ruin tonight for me.*

"The financial arrangements are unusually easy, so we'll be able to close on the house Monday night. I want you to be there."

Kate let out the breath she was holding. The sale of the house was inevitable. It was something she'd been expecting. So why did it still knock the air from her lungs?

"Okay." She labored to pull in a breath.

Elise shook her head. "I think it will be good therapy for you to watch me sign the papers."

"Oh, I'm sure. I can't think of anything I'd rather be doing." She croaked the words from a dry throat, stemming the tide of angry tears that sprang to her eyes. She turned away before her mother could see the effect of her words.

"You'll live through this and be stronger for it," Elise affirmed. "Keep your eyes on the Lord, my dear. He will see you through."

Kate took a deep, steadying breath. "I know. I'm just testy because I haven't found anywhere to live yet. Nothing like the thought of being homeless to shake a person up."

"Jehovah Jireh, God will provide," Mom said serenely. "I'm telling you now so you have time to prepare for it. I know it's still an emotional subject with you." She turned Kate around, her eyes bright with unshed tears of her own. "You can invite Todd to come if you like. He's been very supportive."

"Yeah. Maybe I'll do that." Her mood plunged into the darkness.

Elise embraced her and kissed her gently on the cheek. "Now forget all about moving and go enjoy your evening with that young man of yours. We can talk over the details later. Todd will be here soon."

Kate scuffed from the room, her head bowed. No matter how many times she tried to face the issue, it still hurt to give up this house. And now her mother was asking her to watch her hand it over to the new owners. She hadn't even found a place to live. She'd put it out of her mind once that townhouse across from Todd had been denied her. She supposed she felt that somehow God would work something out for her.

But he hadn't come through. And now her evening was ruined, never mind her future. How was she supposed to have a good time with Todd with this big, dark cloud hanging over her head? Not even shimmying into the gorgeous satin and lace creation she'd once bought on impulse but never worn could improve her mood.

Kate refused to look at herself in the mirror before she left the bedroom, no matter how much Elizabeth pleaded, groveled, and begged. She didn't need anything else to depress her, and her Katie the Whale reflection wouldn't help.

Todd rang the doorbell at five minutes before the hour. Kate swung the door open before the chime was finished ringing and flung herself into his arms.

He looked surprised but quickly regained his composure, wrapping one thick arm around her shoulders and giving her full access to his chest. "I'm glad to see you, too, sweetheart, but I sure didn't expect this kind of reception," he joked.

Kate didn't laugh. But she did straighten up, realizing she was probably getting all that expensive makeup on his starched white shirt.

She realized belatedly that he was dressed in a crisp black pinstriped suit, complete with a snappy red tie. It was the first time she'd seen him in a regular tie, and it somehow exacerbated the situation. Tonight he wasn't Father Todd who worked with her. He was Todd Jensen the man, and looking handsomer than ever.

"Just take me away from here," she grumbled, taking his hand. *Thank God for Todd,* she thought as she realized how much she'd grown to depend on him. He certainly cut a dashing figure—a real Prince Charming to the rescue.

"With pleasure, sweetheart. Right this way." He gestured to the street, where a pink Cadillac awaited them.

"That's odd," she mumbled under her breath.

"What's odd?" he asked, his voice laced with concern.

"Oh, nothing, really. It's just that this car looks remarkably like—"

He opened the passenger door, and she slid in. A thin gold cross hung from the rearview mirror. "Todd, this is my mother's car!" she exclaimed.

"Well, of course it is," he said, seating himself and turning the key in the ignition. "You didn't think I made a habit of driving around in a pink Caddy, did you? Bad for the image."

She chuckled despite her black mood.

He rolled down the window and waved his arm at Elise and Elizabeth, who were peering out the front screen. "Thanks, ladies, for all your help!" he called, then rolled up the window and pulled out onto the street.

"So they were in on this with you," she accused as she settled back into the seat.

Todd tossed a grin at her. "I'll admit I had help," he said. "And your mother and Elizabeth were the best. But every last bit of tonight comes straight from the heart. My heart."

Kate sighed and closed her eyes, leaning her head back against the leather seat. Again, Todd had amazed her, bringing her mind off her problems and making her smile. She'd never loved him as much as she did at this moment, as his eyes spoke volumes even though his tongue was silent, making her feel like royalty just by being there with him.

"I've ordered us a sparkling cider to go with dinner," he commented, watching the road. "So we can have a toast."

"What are we toasting?"

"You. We're toasting you, Kate," he said, his voice gruff with emotion.

"How about toasting the both of us?" She laughed nervously, even more so when she realized how it sounded—as if she were pairing them off.

"We'll toast both of us," he agreed, his lazy smile back in place.

It took only minutes to arrive at Le Petit Chateau, and Kate felt a thrill of excitement when she saw where Todd was taking her. Her limited experience with French food had made it her favorite, but she'd never eaten a meal in a restaurant as glamorous as this one clearly was.

Todd came around to help her out of the car, then took both her hands in his. "Kate, you're so beautiful. That dress…your hair…"

He didn't seem to be able to complete a sentence. He looked her up and down, his gaze igniting a flame in her heart.

She flinched under his scrutiny. Her dress was too tight,

exposing every imperfection to his wandering eye. The high lace collar probably made her look like she had chipmunk cheeks.

But his smile was for her alone. She wished she were the type of woman who could just accept a man's attentions for what they were and not try to read some foul motive into every move, but there it was. She couldn't do that, might never be able to. She'd been analyzing people's reactions to her for years, knowing the best defense was a good offense. So afraid of being hurt, she'd also missed the thrill of a man's eyes on her and her alone.

But Todd was different. She'd known that for weeks now. She could trust him. And he wanted to be with her. She smiled and took the arm he offered. Tonight she wasn't going to psychoanalyze anything. Tonight she was going to be a woman out with the man she loved.

"You look mah-velous, dah-link," she whispered as they walked into the restaurant.

He leaned down and playfully brushed his lips against her cheek. "It's all for you."

Her heartbeat skyrocketed, and she looked away. Funny how his mere presence could cause such a reaction inside her. She felt as if she were floating.

His preparations had obviously not ceased with enlisting Elizabeth's help and borrowing her mother's car, for they were greeted by the maître d' as if they'd been regulars for years. It was no surprise, then, that they were led to a cozy corner booth, lit only with the flickering light of a crystal chandelier and the single candle burning on their table.

~ ~ ~ ~ ~

Todd waited for her reaction, not even realizing he was holding his breath as he did so. He hadn't been breathing evenly since Kate stepped out the door and into his arms.

She was, indeed, breathtakingly beautiful. The dress was nice, but it was her full, rosy face that caught his greatest attention. Her eyes were so large and luminescent that his heart flipped over every time he looked at her. He wanted to kiss her. And tonight, he would. He'd take her in his arms and kiss her long and soundly.

Finally. It seemed he'd been waiting an eternity for this moment. Now here it was, and he wasn't sure how to proceed. He slipped a hand into his jacket pocket, feeling for the reassuring shape of the velvet box he carried there.

Father, please give me the words to say to make Kate my own.

His sister was praying for him, he knew. Probably Elizabeth and Kate's mother, too. Praying and speculating on the outcome of this evening.

I won't disappoint them, he thought with a smile. *Tonight is the night.*

Fifteen

The menu was in French, and Todd translated for her, ordering for them both when they'd made their selections. He chose the pheasant Champaubert and Kate the fillet of sole Véronique, each wanting to try something exotic on such a special evening.

They talked quietly as they ate. He couldn't keep his eyes off her, though she often looked shyly away. He couldn't believe God would give him such a lovely woman for a wife, and he thanked God over and over as they ate.

He'd settled on the perfect opening for a marriage proposal. He'd simply ask her if she'd found a place to live, and when she said she hadn't found anything he'd suggest they get married so she could move in with him. Tam would be in school by the time they made all the wedding arrangements. He wanted Kate to have the wedding of her dreams, but he didn't want to wait any longer than necessary to make her his wife.

But he was getting ahead of himself. He had to ask her first.

"Have you found a place to live yet?" he asked between bites of a melt-in-your-mouth strawberry crêpe.

The atmosphere at the table went from sunshine to ice in one moment. Todd was surprised the candle didn't snuff out with the chilly breeze that rent the air. Kate froze with her fork halfway to her mouth. A shadow crossed her face and then disappeared, replaced by a forced calm.

The moment was shattered. And somehow he was responsible.

"What?" he queried gently. "What did I say?"

She tried to smile, but her mouth quivered, so she thinned her lips to a straight line. "Nothing's wrong. Let's just eat."

"Kate." He reached his hand across the table, palm up.

She stared at it for a full minute before placing her hand in his, but when she did, she gave it a reassuring squeeze.

"I wasn't going to bring this up tonight. You've gone to all this trouble, and—"

His heart nearly stopped beating in his chest as his love for her welled. He wanted to protect her, cherish her. "You can tell me anything, Kate. You know that. And I'll try to help if I can."

"I wouldn't be so quick to bite," she grumbled, shoving a forkful of crêpe into her mouth and chewing rapidly. "It might be more than you want to chew."

"Try me." At the moment, he was ready to slay dragons, leap tall buildings in a single bound. All she had to do was say the word.

"You might run the risk of being bored to death," she warned.

He chuckled.

"Mom is closing on the house Monday evening. And she wants me to be there to see the dirty deed. Can you imagine? Whoever said life was fair?"

"I'm sorry," he said, squeezing her hand. He met her gaze, expecting to see tears and sadness, but instead was surprised to see light. Her eyes were soft, and clear as a new spring day. There was strength lurking in those amber depths, and once more Todd's heart clinched.

She smiled, and this time it was the genuine article. He couldn't help but smile in return.

"I should be the one apologizing. You've gone all out to create this wonderful evening, and here I am singing sad songs and spoiling the mood."

"You're not—" he began, but she cut him off with a finger to her lips.

"Let's not talk about houses or moving or anything else having to do with real life tonight. Can we just sit back, enjoy the music, and talk nonsense?"

"Gladly," he agreed, picking up his champagne glass and tipping it to her. *As long as you don't think a marriage proposal is nonsense!*

Slowly, so she wouldn't notice, he moved his hand to his side and patted his pocket protectively. *Anytime now,* he coached himself with a secretive smile. He'd just have to figure out a different approach. One that would set the stage better than his first attempt.

Kate leaned back in the seat, watching the dance floor. Several couples moved slowly across the floor in time to a waltz. The scene was elegant and refined, and for a moment she wished she could be a part of the picture.

"Care to dance, *mademoiselle?*"

She hadn't realized Todd had moved, but he was standing behind her chair, leaning over to whisper the tantalizing words in her ear. His breath was warm and sent a shiver of delight through her, even as panic gripped her lower extremities.

He pulled her chair back and waited for her to stand. Evidently, she thought dryly, the question was rhetorical.

And why shouldn't she dance with him? This was her night, a night dreams were made of. It was about time she traded in her nightmares for happily-ever-after. She smiled and extended her hand, enjoying his admiring glance as she stood to her feet. How it happened she'd never know, but somehow she was dressed to the nines in an expensive restaurant with the handsomest man in the world by her side. A man she loved more than breathing. And it felt great.

She nearly floated to the dance floor on Todd's arm, but apparently she wasn't floating high enough off the ground, for she suddenly stumbled over someone's very large foot. Kate's world tilted, but Todd caught her in his strong arms before she fell. She closed her eyes and gripped his sleeve, mortified that she'd made such a spectacle of herself.

She sighed. *You can dress her up, but you can't take her out.* She was a living, walking—well, *trying* to walk—cliché! The foot belonged to a young man not a day over twenty, Kate surmised. And he was laughing—at her, apparently.

Todd didn't seem to notice. His eyes were glued to her, concern evident on his face. She shrugged and smiled for his benefit, but she couldn't help the way her stomach tightened at the young man's laughter. She struggled to regain her mental equilibrium. Maybe the kid was laughing at himself for being so clumsy. He'd offered a muttered apology when he pulled his foot back under the table where it belonged.

And even if he was laughing at her, what difference did it make? She was here with Todd, and he liked her. He knew the real Kate Logan, with all her bumps and bruises, and he liked her anyway.

So there, her mind countered as she relaxed into Todd's embrace. He was a good dancer, light on his feet. And he knew how to waltz. For a man who tended to rely on book learning, he was amazingly adept. It was on the tip of her tongue to ask if a book could teach her to dance so well.

Kate hadn't danced since…well, for a long time, so to say she was a little rusty in her skills would be a severe understatement. But in Todd's arms, she found she didn't have the slightest bit of trouble following the steps. She merely had to relax in his embrace and let him lead her around the floor.

Her satin smooth emerald gown swirled as they spun, and

Kate gloried in the feeling. She remembered as a little girl "testing" her dresses in front of Daddy to find the ones that spun the best. This gown would most definitely have passed muster, she thought gleefully.

And so would Todd. Dad would have respected him—liked him, even—though her father had threatened never to let a man darken the door where his only daughter was concerned. She wished he could be here to see his daughter in the arms of a godly, loving man. It would have made his heart proud and set his mind at ease.

"Penny for your thoughts," Todd whispered, his lips brushing against the tender skin of her neck. "No…make that a million dollars. Your thoughts are worth at least that much to me."

Her breath caught in her throat. His eyes were so dark that they appeared almost black in the light. Black and glimmering.

"I was just thinking about my father. Wishing he could be here to meet you," she said, surprised that she could find her voice past the lump in her throat.

"I'd have liked that." His low, rich voice sent tendrils of warmth down her spine.

"He'd have liked *you*," she whispered back, her breath spiraling down to an even pace just as the song ended.

They stopped and clapped, waiting for the next song to start. Feeling suddenly nervous with Todd, she took a moment to look around, careful to avoid the area where the young man who'd tripped her was sitting.

Her gaze was drawn to an obviously wealthy woman who looked about Kate's age. Dressed in a shimmering white sequined gown, the slim blonde had a flawless complexion, elegantly coiffured hair, and long enameled nails. In short, she was everything Kate always wanted to be. Or at least, everything she'd wanted to be until tonight. For once, she was happy just being plain old Kate Logan, albeit the dressed-up version.

Still, she couldn't help but watch the woman as the next song, a slow ballad, started and Todd once again took her in his arms. To her relief, he didn't try to speak but left her alone with her thoughts.

The blonde was decked out in diamonds. Several necklaces hung at her neck. Giant diamond clips graced her tiny ears. And her hands were covered with diamond rings. Kate wondered if she had been born to money or had married it. The woman was sitting with a middle-aged, potbellied man with a cigar dangling from his lips. The wrinkled skin around his forehead and eyes bespoke both his age and his mood. Kate shivered, glad money wasn't a temptation for her.

The blonde woman looked up, and their eyes met. The woman's eyes widened slightly as she took stock of Kate's dress. Raising one chic eyebrow, she pursed her lips and leaned toward the man she was with, gesturing toward Kate and saying something behind her napkin that made them both laugh.

The man looked Kate over, shaking his head with a sneer on his lips. He replied to the woman, and they both laughed again. Todd's dance steps turned her away then, but it was too late.

Kate could no more help the panic that enveloped her than she could make herself model thin overnight. Darkness closed in on her. The comfort of Todd's embrace suddenly turned to the arms of a vise, constricting her, holding her captive when she wanted desperately to flee. She knew full well what the couple were sneering at. She looked like a big green balloon, and she had *country bumpkin* written all over her. She didn't belong here. She didn't belong with a man like Todd.

Could he tell she'd stuffed herself into her dress? Was he

embarrassed to be seen with her? Did he realize people were laughing at them?

Her eyes darted from table to table, her stomach clenching in spasms as she noted the number of people watching the dance floor. Some of them were laughing. Were they laughing at her?

Her gaze inadvertently landed on the young man who'd tripped her. His legs stretched out from underneath the table again, and he was leering at her.

Wasn't he?

Her head started to spin, and she squeezed her eyes closed, leaning her head against the solid wall of Todd's chest. She tried to focus on his strong, steady heartbeat, on his gentle humming in her ears, but she couldn't shut the nightmare memory from her mind.

"It's time for our dance." Devan Davis's voice was rough and cocky, but Kate didn't mind. This was the moment she'd waited for all her life. She'd never been popular. Kids had always teased her about her weight. But tonight, against all odds, she'd been announced the homecoming queen.

And Devan Davis was waiting to dance with her.

Her mother had helped her pick out a dress and do her hair. Tonight, she felt pretty. And she must be, to be named homecoming queen.

Devan was moving too fast for a slow song, and he didn't put his arms around her as she'd seen other prom kings do.

Instead, he was laughing at her, and suddenly she noticed the crowd of kids around her.

"Look at what I caught…a whale!" It was Devan's voice piercing through her haze.

"It's Katie the Whale."

"Look at Queen Blubber."

"Did she really think she got voted queen because she's popular? What a joke!"

Joke's on you, Katie the Whale.

It was as if all of the people who'd taunted and gibed her over the years were there, jeering in unison, their voices swelling with each second that passed. Reed-thin cheerleaders, kids at the homecoming dance, classmates in second-grade gymnastics.

I'm afraid she's going to get hurt, Mrs. Logan. It would be best for her to withdraw from the team.

"Kate. Kate, sweetheart." Todd's voice was gentle in her ear, coaxing her from her thoughts. Her heart still hammered so hard it hurt, and her lungs burned from forgetting to breathe.

"What's wrong? You're so tense all of a sudden. Did I step on your toes?" he teased.

Her blank look disturbed him. He'd been lost in thought, planning again how to word his proposal, when he'd felt her stiffen in his arms. "Katie, love, are you all right?"

When he said her name, she jumped as if hit with a bolt of electricity. She took in a great gulp of air and wrenched herself from his grasp.

He clenched his jaw and let her go. What else could he do?

"I'm sorry. Todd, I'm so...sorry!" She hiccuped the last word, then bolted from the dance floor like a green-broke filly under a saddle for the first time.

What was happening? What was she doing? Hurt and anger warred in his chest. Stunned, he watched as Kate made a bee-line for the exit, not even stopping at the table to retrieve her purse. By the time he'd gathered his wits enough to pick up the tab, collect their things, and follow her out the door, she was gone.

He hoped she'd caught a cab. There was no sign of her in

any direction, but he drove around for an hour afterward just to be sure.

Then he drove to her house to return the car, but most of all to check on Kate. If she wasn't home, he was going to call out a full-blown search, starting with her mother. He was, after all, responsible for this.

He breathed a sigh of relief as he pulled into the driveway. Kate's bedroom light was on. She was safe, at least, even if she wouldn't ever speak to him again. Reluctantly he put his truck into gear and drove back to his home, going straight to his room and slamming the door behind him.

Pain seared his chest. He didn't know what had happened back at the restaurant, but one thing was certain. He'd been jilted. And oh, how it hurt.

It was almost physical agony to kneel by his bed, but he did it nonetheless. He needed wisdom far beyond what he was capable of on his own.

Oh, Father, what do I do now?

Sixteen

K ate didn't sleep Saturday night for crying and praying. She finally fell into a fitful doze sometime in the
early hours of the morning. Her heart wasn't breaking. In fact, she doubted whether she even had a heart. She
certainly couldn't feel it.

No one had to tell her she'd lost the best thing that had ever
happened to her. Todd would never speak to her again, and
with good reason. *She* would never speak to herself again if she
could somehow manage it. But despite her best efforts, her
mind churned along, replaying the events of the prior evening
in agonizing, gruesome detail.

How could she have been so foolish? She couldn't believe
she had acted so immaturely. Running out on Todd like that
was inexcusable. It plunged past rude and into desperate. Her
cheeks flushed with embarrassment every time she thought
about it.

Poor Todd. It would be a blow to any man's ego to be
dumped on like that, even if the dumper was Katie the Whale.
Especially so.

That she hurt Todd bothered her worse than her own
shame. She'd seen the flicker of anger in his eyes when she
wrenched away from him and ran off. She obviously didn't
know the meaning of true love. True love didn't hurt the
beloved one but only uplifted and edified him.

Love is kind. She hadn't been kind last night. She'd been
unthinking and cruel. With Christ as her example, she knew
she fell far short. Truth be told, she didn't even show up on the
scale. After all the kindness and generosity Todd had shown,

she had repaid him with evil for good.

He might even resign from Wedding Works. Why would he want the strain of working with her day in and day out on a regular basis?

Her pulse pounded in her skull. She trudged toward the kitchen and a good stout cup of coffee, hoping her mother was still sleeping. She didn't know if she was up to the inevitable interrogation. And they still needed to discuss the imminent move and closing on the house.

She was determined not to answer the phone either. If talking to her mother sounded bad, a conversation with Elizabeth would be ten times worse. Right now, Kate was too humiliated to show her face to anyone. Though she hadn't missed a Sunday service in years, she couldn't bring herself to get dressed, much less leave the house.

As much as she needed to worship God, commune with her heavenly Father, there was no way she could go to church without seeing Thomas and Elizabeth. And that was enough to keep her away. She prayed God would forgive her. Instead, she decided, she would hibernate the day away and lick her self-inflicted wounds.

The doorbell rang, and she jumped.

But of course it wouldn't be Todd. It couldn't be. He wouldn't dare come here after last night. Would he?

She dashed to the door but hesitated with her hand on the knob. Instead, she shifted toward the peephole, holding her breath as if the person on the other side might be able to guess her furtive action.

She couldn't help that her heart beat faster or that hope sprang new with the morning.

Please, please, Lord, let it be Todd.

She pinched one eye closed and peeked through the looking

glass. Two burly, uniformed men were on the other side of the door, and in the street behind them she could see a moving van.

The breath left her lungs as if she had had the wind knocked out of her. A moving van. How quickly she'd forgotten.

"Are they here already?" Elise Logan's voice came from the kitchen. But Kate had just come from the kitchen, and her mother hadn't been there when she left. She had assumed Elise was still asleep in her bedroom.

She whirled to find her mother entering the living room, dressed like a commercial for a health and fitness gym. Pink Spandex everything, with a headband to match. She held a one-pound weight in each hand and was still pumping her arms methodically up and down.

"Mother! What are you doing?" A worried frown furrowed her brow. All she could think of was her mother's MS and what overdoing exercise might do to inflame her symptoms.

"Relax, Kate. I was just taking my morning walk. I've been working up to two miles, day by day. Just today I added these weights." She waved them in her fists for emphasis.

"I didn't know you were walking," Kate said, trying to keep her tone light. "I should be joining you."

"And I should have asked you to. I'm sorry. You've been so preoccupied lately. I've been trying to get my muscles back into circulation so I can learn to play golf when I get to Roseborough."

Kate had forgotten the men behind the door until the bell rang again. "I suppose we should answer the door," she said glumly.

"Oh, cheer up, dear. We'll close on the house tomorrow, and then this big burden will be off your shoulders. You'll be surprised how quickly your concentration will turn to that handsome chaplain of yours."

Kate didn't bother to correct her. Instead, she whirled back around and opened the door to the moving men.

It didn't take them long to clear out the living room. Without furniture, the room looked vacant and void. *Like her heart.*

She spent a half hour watching the movers and then returned to the garage, scrubbing her vanity with sandpaper to drown out the noise of the men. The ugly puce paint was gone, replaced by a hardwood finish with a lovely swirling grain. She was using a fine-grain paper now to do the finishing sanding. Maybe she'd even polyurethane it today when her sanding was complete. The vanity, at least, was one part of her life that she hadn't been wrong about and hadn't completely ruined.

It was small consolation for a future that looked empty and bleak. She'd always known she'd be alone. She'd just never known the extent of what she was missing.

Now she knew.

Among other things, the movers left her the kitchen table. Her mother wouldn't need it, since her apartment came installed with a breakfast nook. Then again, maybe the kitchen table was really being left so she'd have someplace to sit when they closed on the house. At this point, she didn't have anywhere to move the stupid table to, never mind the couch and the other sundry furniture stored in an extra bedroom so the movers wouldn't get confused about what should go and what should stay.

The doorbell rang again. Not knowing where Elise was, or if she'd even heard it, Kate sighed and dusted off her jeans. Why the movers had shut the door and locked themselves out was beyond her, but she couldn't keep them waiting all day.

To her surprise, the door wasn't shut. In fact, the screen door was wired open to make it easier for the movers to carry out large pieces of furniture. Instead, she found a delivery man standing at the door holding a large bouquet of red roses.

Her heart soared, then dropped. Why would she be receiving flowers from Todd now? And no one but Todd could have sent them. He must have ordered them yesterday. A lump formed deep in her throat and finally, belatedly, a dull pain began in her chest.

At least she could feel again. She took the bouquet and asked the delivery man to wait while she procured a tip from her purse in her bedroom. Secretly, she just wanted time to read the card.

As soon as she was out of sight of the door, she heedlessly tossed the bouquet onto her bed and snatched up the card.

It was a simple message. *All my love, Todd.* So she did have a heart after all. She felt it rip in two as she read and reread the words.

She took a deep breath, scrambled for her wallet, and dashed back out to the waiting delivery man. The flowers were from a small, independently owned shop. Maybe the man could tell her something about this delivery.

She handed him a large tip, wondering how best to broach the subject. Her mind hit a blank, but when he turned to go, she exclaimed aloud, causing him to turn back. Even if she appeared foolish, she had to put herself out of her misery.

"Ma'am?" he asked politely.

"I was wondering…" she said, wiping her damp palms on her jeans, "if you might happen to know when these flowers were ordered?"

"Why, sure, ma'am. Took the order myself." He gave her a friendly wink. "That young man of yours is one of my best customers, thanks to you."

Kate chuckled hoarsely.

"He ordered these here flowers just this morning, ma'am. Couldn't have been more than two minutes after I was open, and here's my phone ringing clear off the hook!"

"He ordered them this morning? Sunday morning?" she repeated, certain she must have heard him wrong.

"Yes, ma'am. Yer feller is a good 'un, he is. A good 'un for sure."

Todd sat behind his desk in Thomas's basement, his hands folded sedately on top. He'd rearranged the piles of papers cluttering his desk four times, and it still looked every bit as messy as it had before. He'd come to try to catch up on some paperwork and get his mind off his disaster of a date, but so far he had done neither.

The memory of Kate's large, luminescent amber eyes clouded his vision. It couldn't be over. It just couldn't. How could he live without her? He wadded up the nearest piece of paper and tossed it into the trash can with a growl.

"Todd?" came Thomas's voice from the doorway.

He squeezed his eyes shut. Company. Just what he didn't need right now. It was a mistake coming here. He'd been certain everyone would be at church.

He straightened his shoulders and swiveled around in his chair. "Good morning, Thomas," he said, hoping his voice didn't sound as low and churlish as he felt.

"You're not at church," Thomas said, surprised.

"No, I'm not." Todd ran a hand across his jaw, realizing what a sight he must make. He knew his eyes were red rimmed, and he hadn't felt like shaving.

"Whoa, buddy, you look awful."

"Thanks for the compliment."

"You want to talk about it?" Thomas rolled Kate's desk chair over next to Todd and sat down, leaning his elbows on his knees.

No. Not really. What Todd wanted was for Thomas to be magically transported to the South Pole, but that wasn't going to happen. And it wasn't Thomas's fault his life was a shambles. "It's nothing," he said aloud.

"I understand if you don't want to yak at me," Thomas said, leaning back in his chair. "Talking is a girl thing, right?"

Todd experienced the lightning-hot inner jolt before he could get control of his expression, and he knew Thomas had seen it, too. He shrugged and grinned.

"Kate." It wasn't a question.

"More like *not* Kate," Todd said miserably. "She dumped me."

"That doesn't sound like the woman I know. She's pretty much gone where you're concerned."

"You can say that again."

"Poor choice of words." Thomas chuckled. "I meant she loves you. Has for some time, really."

"I thought she returned my feeling," Todd agreed. "Or at least until last night. I think maybe we were all reading emotion into Kate's actions where none was meant."

"Me, I could be way off base," Thomas said. "But Elizabeth knows. And she's never wrong about this kind of stuff. Besides, you know how women talk."

"Do you think…?"

"That there's a chance for you? I'd bet my next paycheck." His eyes widened as he realized what he'd said, and he quickly added, "If I were a betting man, that is. Which I'm definitely not."

"Relax, Thomas. I'm not going to snitch your secret faults to God."

Thomas blew out a breath and smiled. "Glad to hear it. Can I give you some advice?"

"You've known Kate a lot longer than I have. I'd appreciate any help. I'm at a complete loss, myself."

"Then don't give up on her."

"Oh, I didn't plan to."

Thomas chuckled. "Then fight for her. Take the brakes off. She's stubborn, and it may take her a while to listen. But go knock her door down."

"With my bare hands?"

"If necessary. I'd suggest a crowbar. Quicker and cleaner, if you know what I mean. And you can threaten her with it if need be, to get her to listen."

"That sounds more like Elizabeth than Kate," Todd commented.

"You've got that right," Thomas agreed, laughing loudly. "Even a crowbar won't keep that woman at bay."

"At least you're trying," Todd said, standing. "Which is more than I've done this morning."

"That's the spirit," Thomas cheered.

"Beat her door down, huh?"

"Do it!"

Todd shook his head and grinned. At least he had something productive to do instead of moping around the office. And maybe Thomas was right. Maybe it was time to take the brakes off this relationship.

Monday morning found Todd slumped in front of the kitchen table, a pile of dollar bills in front of him on the right and an open phone book on the left. He glared at the offending bills and scratched at his unshaven face.

"What's up, big bro?" Tam asked, pouring herself a cup of coffee. "You look like a little kid robbing his piggy bank."

"Pretty much," he said, groaning. "This is all that's left of the emergency money I had stashed away." He scowled and ruffled his hand through his hair. "And it's not enough."

"Enough for what?"

Todd scowled again. "I was trying to send Kate more flowers."

"More flowers? You sent her flowers then?" Tam looked pleased with herself.

"Six times," he groused.

"In the past two days?"

"Three days. Two bouquets on Saturday. Three yesterday. And one this morning. And I was going to send her another one, but I don't have enough money." He slumped forward, his chin resting on his palm.

"I'll lend you the money," she said, chuckling. "But don't you think you might be overdoing it? Six flower arrangements seems a bit excessive even to me. I'm sure she's gotten the message that you're head over heels for her by now."

Todd stood so suddenly his chair tipped backward and crashed to the floor. He jabbed a hand through the ragged ends of his hair and made a deep, guttural sound.

"That's just it. She doesn't know. I called her twenty-two times yesterday, and she won't even pick up the phone!"

Tam put an arm around his shoulders, making soothing, motherly clucking sounds. "Did something happen while I was away this weekend that I'm not aware of?" she queried gently.

He blew out an angry, frustrated breath. The last thing he wanted to do was discuss his love life with his sister. Then again, she was the only woman around. Maybe she'd know what to do.

"I took her to dinner. A nice dinner." He laughed coldly. "I was planning to pop the question."

He ignored Tam's surprised exclamation and continued. He didn't want pity. What he needed was advice. He would get Kate back or die trying. Life with out her was too miserable even to contemplate.

"Everything was going great. We ate dinner and dessert and then went down to the floor to dance. And then..." He paused and swiped a hand down his face, muttering under his breath.

Tam waited without speaking, giving his arm a reassuring squeeze.

"And then," he continued, "she wigged out on me. One second we were dancing, and the next she was bolting from the restaurant like her dress was on fire. And I don't know why!" His voice continued to rise in volume until he was nearly shouting. "I don't know what I did wrong!"

"Maybe it's not you," Tam suggested gently. "Maybe it's her."

"She's wonderful, Tam. She's vibrant and pretty and gentle. And she's got such a kind, giving heart. I've never met another woman like her."

"You don't have to convince me, Todd. I know any woman who could catch my brother's attention would have to be special. The question is, does she know all these things?"

"I was going to tell her Saturday night!" he yelled, slamming his fist against the tabletop.

"And you've tried to call, but she won't answer. Have you tried going to see her?"

Todd hung his head. "No. If she doesn't want to see me, I don't want to make things worse for her by showing up on her doorstep."

"Todd Andrew Jensen, don't you dare give up on this special lady!"

"I'm not!" he defended, bristling. "I've been sending her flowers practically every hour on the hour." He glared at the phone book. "Or at least I was until I ran out of money. I'm just about ready to get a credit card and charge up a mountain of debt," he said without humor. "I don't want to dig into my savings, or we won't have a honeymoon. Of course, if I don't have a bride, I guess that's a moot point."

"I'm glad your sense of humor is intact," Tam said. "Listen, I'll give you the money you need if you really think it will help. But may I offer another suggestion first? Something that might not bankrupt you?"

He forced a smile for Tam's sake. She really was trying, and it was clear how much she loved him. If only she could delve into the female psyche and help him figure Kate out. "I'm listening," he said gruffly.

"You'd better sit down," she said, gesturing to the chair he'd tipped over. "This could take a while."

Seventeen

W ith six flower arrangements in her room, Kate barely had room to maneuver. The red roses contrasted nicely with the powder blue paint on her walls, at least. But if he sent so much as one more bouquet, she would have to find closet space to display them.

The house echoed with emptiness. Her mother had moved out right along with the furniture, giving Kate a cheery peck on the cheek and telling her to call if she needed anything. Without her mother there, it wasn't really a home. The emptiness resounded in Kate's mind. It was the reason she'd placed all the flowers in her room. The rest of the house was so lonely and bare.

She sighed and resigned herself to the evening ahead. There was no chance Todd would be there to help her, so she had to face the lions, as it were, on her own. She wasn't frightened or melancholy. The funny thing was, she didn't seem to feel anything, as if selling her childhood home weren't a momentous occasion and one to be dreaded.

Without Todd, not much of anything mattered. But she hadn't accepted any of his phone calls, and that alone tormented her. Yesterday, every time she started to relax, the phone would ring. Thank goodness for Caller ID. It felt like a dagger slicing through her chest every time she checked the box and saw *Jensen, Fr. T* on it. He'd certainly shown how persistent he could be when he wanted something. The question was, what *did* he want? That was why she hadn't answered the phone. She was so afraid he was calling to resign his position as chaplain that she thought it better not to talk with him at all.

And what would she say to him? *I'm sorry* just didn't cover her multitude of sins. Begging and pleading wouldn't help. So, in her own special brand of denial, she refused to pick up the phone.

Today, however, there had been only one delivery of flowers and no more phone calls. She wondered if he was giving up. She hoped he was. If he decided to keep the job, maybe they could eventually work things out.

Yeah, right. And the moon is made of green cheese.

She glanced at the kitchen wall to check the time, but of course the clock had gone with her mother. She grumbled to herself and checked her watch. In fifteen minutes, the new owners of this home would be here. She didn't have much to prepare. Flip the switch on the coffeemaker and pull down a bag of store-bought cookies, and she was ready. There wasn't any furniture to dust, and Mom had run the vacuum before she'd left.

Kate smoothed down her rayon skirt and adjusted the collar of her silk blouse, wishing she could wear sweats and get away with it. She was uncomfortable enough in this house without having to dress for business. Especially unpleasant business.

She couldn't even sit on the couch to wait, and she didn't feel like sprawling on the floor. Finally she slumped into a kitchen chair in a huff.

Soon it would be over. Tomorrow she would start looking in earnest for a new place to live. She might very well have to take the first place that was offered to her, but that wouldn't be so bad. She could make long-range plans after the desperate pain in her chest lessened to a dull ache.

If and when that ever happened.

The doorbell rang. Kate jumped from the seat, startled, and rushed to the coffeepot, flipping the switch to turn it on. Running a hand over her hair to make sure it was in place, she glanced at her watch. The new owners were ten minutes early.

She took a deep breath and swung the door open. Her heart turned over, and over yet again, making her feel as if she were on one of those roller coasters that did several loop-de-loops in rapid succession.

Todd stood on the doorstep, dressed impeccably in black clericals and a wool sport coat, a smile on his face and a single red rose extended in his hand.

Her first impulse was to slam the door in his face and make a run for her bedroom, dive under the covers, and never come out again. But of course that was impossible, not to mention rude. Still, she couldn't help the exclamation that left her lips at his sudden appearance. "Todd, what are you doing here?"

Todd cringed inside, but kept his face calm and his heartbeat level. She wasn't overjoyed to see him. That much was obvious. But that didn't matter. He was here, and he wasn't taking no for an answer. He knew how hard this night was going to be for her, and there was no way he was going to stand by and let her go through it alone just because of some giant misunderstanding. He was convinced that was what it must be.

He'd prayed all night for direction, but his heart was unwilling to give Kate up. He took that as an indication from God that their relationship was meant to be. That and his sister's suggestion to bring her, in person, a single red rose as a symbol of his devotion. It sounded a little corny to him, but if it worked, it would be worth it.

Unfortunately, she didn't faint at his feet in blatant ardor at the sight of his meager peace offering. The scowl creasing her brow was definitely not the reaction he was hoping for.

When he didn't answer her question, Kate raised one eyebrow and crossed her arms as an afterthought. She was so beautiful. Her face flushed becomingly, suggesting a warm and wonderful heart under that cold and crisp business outfit.

He set his jaw. Stubborn was his middle name.

"I'm coming in whether you like it or not, Kate Logan," he ground out through clenched teeth.

Her mouth opened in surprise, and she stepped back from the door as if she'd been physically assaulted.

He took that as an opportunity to charge through the door like a raging bull. But he stopped short just past the foyer. "What happened to your house?"

The place was completely empty. Obviously Elise had moved out, but hadn't she left anything for Kate? Anger seared his chest. No wonder Kate was so upset. Why hadn't she told him about this? The urge to fold her in his arms was strong but was quickly extinguished by one look at the humorless smile on her face.

"Pretty pathetic, isn't it?" she asked dryly. "I'd ask you to sit, but as you can see…"

"That's okay," he said immediately. "I can sit on the floor."

She let out a breath. "You don't have to do that. Mom left me the kitchen table. And six chairs."

He wondered that her mother hadn't left her enough furniture to furnish a townhouse, but then, Kate wouldn't need furniture at all if she married him. "For you," he said, extending the rose to her.

For you? Now there was a slick and debonair line if he'd ever heard one. Maybe Tam wasn't so far off when she called him dunderhead.

He raked his fingers through his hair, his mind awhirl. He'd given a lot of thought to his offensive, how he was going to get into her house. But now that he was here, what was he supposed to do? He supposed he ought to start with *I love you,* but that was kind of an awkward thing just to blurt out. He rather pictured a heady embrace or, at the very least, bending down on one knee.

"Again, I have to ask," she said, interrupting his thoughts. "Why are you here?" She didn't sound angry, just tired. Perhaps she hadn't been able to sleep any better than he had. Every day without her was an eternity.

He patted his coat pocket, where the velvet box was burning a hole. If he was going to do this, he'd best get at it, right here in the middle of the barren living room floor. His pulse pounded in anticipation. But before he could so much as bend a knee, the doorbell sounded. He muffled his verbal reaction with his fist. Of all the lousy timing. The new owners had ruined everything.

He thought he'd planned it so he'd have time to propose and make things right between them—not to mention take that kiss he'd been waiting so long for—and still be available for the closing. Now it appeared that the most important part of this night would have to wait. He resigned himself to the inevitable and turned to Kate.

"Do you want me to get the door for you?" he asked gently.

"If you don't mind."

He moved to the door and swung it open, greeting a smiling couple and the real estate agent with a grin and a hearty handshake. He quickly gathered their names and gave them his own.

It was only when he went to introduce Kate that he turned around to look at her face.

She was swallowing rapidly, weaving back and forth on her

feet. Her face was as white as a sheet. If he didn't know better, he'd think she had seen a ghost.

"Devan Davis." The words were whispered so lightly that only Todd picked up on them. He had no idea who this Devan Davis was, but it was obvious the man upset Kate. He felt his dander rising.

Why did he always want to punch something when he got angry? It certainly wasn't the Christian way of things. He supposed it had something to do with his desire to protect Kate from harm and his inability to do so. He unclenched his hands and forced a smile.

Kate blinked rapidly, as if to clear her head, then cleared her throat and smiled. "If you'll come this way," she said, gesturing toward the kitchen. "My mother should be here any minute, and then we can get started."

Devan, his wife, and the realtor followed Kate into the kitchen. Todd lagged behind, his head spinning.

What did Kate have to do with this man? Why should she be afraid of him? It was fear he saw in her eyes before she shaded them and threw on her facade. Todd racked his brain for an answer, some clue Kate might have dropped in one of their conversations. But he came up blank. He had no clue who Devan Davis was. He'd just have to sit back and wait it out, keeping a close eye on Kate and helping her whenever he could.

Kate's hands trembled slightly as she offered a plate of cookies, though Todd was certain he was the only one who noticed. Devan was openly staring at her, in admiration, as far as Todd could tell. It was a wonder his wife didn't elbow him in the ribs for gawking at another woman.

Todd was hard pressed not to do the elbowing himself. *Mine, mine, mine,* his thoughts echoed, sounding like a toddler with a favorite toy. Only Kate was so much more to him than that.

Devan cleared his throat. "Katie? Katie Logan? Can that be you?"

Kate whirled around and met his gaze head on. "Yes, Devan. It's nice to see you again," she said quietly.

So they did know each other. That solved one riddle. When and where were next on Todd's list.

Devan laughed aloud. "I can't believe it. I just really can't believe *you* are the Katie Logan I knew." He whistled, long and low. "Man, have you changed....I mean, you look really good, Katie."

Todd readied his fist. It appeared he was, indeed, going to have to knock this man senseless. He couldn't say that he minded. His blood was pounding through his head like a bass drum.

"It's Kate now, Devan," she said. She smiled, but Todd could see her mouth quivering. "I...if you'll excuse me for one moment?"

She put a mug of coffee in front of each of them, then smoothed her skirt with her palms, smiled again, and walked out of the kitchen.

Todd caught the realtor's eye and held up his index finger. "It'll be just a minute, ladies. And gentleman," he said, as if it were an afterthought. *Gentleman,* Todd thought, *is a little presumptuous for this guy.*

He walked quietly down the hall, thinking Kate might have gone to her bedroom to regroup. Feeling like a thief, he entered quietly and made a quick survey of the room. He counted six floral arrangements, and his heart was warmed. At least she hadn't thrown them away in her anger.

A newly varnished hardwood vanity took up the middle of

the floor, set on a bunch of old, spread out newspapers. He could still smell the fresh odor of the stain and finish. It was a pretty piece, obviously antique. He wondered if Kate had refinished it herself.

The only thing he didn't see was Kate. He left the room and went back down the hall, noting the extra bedroom stuffed full of furniture. So Elise hadn't left her daughter without furniture after all. That was one less thing to worry about.

Thinking she might have returned to the kitchen, he was headed in that direction when he saw a light in the crack under the bathroom door.

Great. He could hardly barge in there. He felt his face flush with embarrassment. He had to know what was going on, even if he discovered he was interrupting a personal trip to the john.

He knocked quietly. "Kate, are you in there?"

Duh. Where else would she be? Certainly not in the kitchen with Devan the slick of tongue.

He heard her mumble something, but the door remained closed. "Will you let me in?"

Now he was going beyond personal. He knew his face was as red as the roses he sent. He gritted his teeth and plunged on. "I just want to make sure you're all right."

The door cracked open, and he saw one wary amber eye peering out at him.

"What do you really want?" she whispered.

"Just what I said. To make sure you're okay. You looked a little peaked when that Devan fellow showed up. I was worried."

"About me?" She actually sounded surprised. "That's very sweet, Todd. But as you can see, I'm okay."

He chuckled. "All I can see is one eye. What can I tell from that?"

"Well, it isn't bloodshot, is it?" she asked, answering his chuckle with her own.

"No, you've got me there. But I'd feel a good deal better if I could see your whole face. Humor your poor chaplain on this, will you please?"

She gave a melodramatic sigh and opened the door wide. "There, see? There's nothing to worry about. Satisfied?"

"No, not really." Grabbing her by the waist, he pushed her back into the bathroom and shut the door behind them, locking it firmly.

Her eyes widened in alarm when the lock clicked into place, but at least her face had regained its color.

"What are you doing?" she hissed, laughter bubbling in her chest. She couldn't believe he'd just shoved her into the bathroom and locked the door behind them.

"We," he said, a dangerous gleam in his eye, "are going to hash this out, right here and right now." It relieved him to know she wasn't afraid of him. But he wanted more. So much more. And he wasn't waiting one more second to get what he'd come for.

Eighteen

T odd, I have guests waiting! We have to close on the house! I think that's my mother's voice I hear." Kate's heart began pounding in her chest, matching the soaring rhythm of her mind.

"Good. Then she can take care of things. Or they can wait." His tone brooked no argument. He leaned back against the bathroom door as if seeking assurance that she would not flee.

"I'm not running away this time," she said, squaring her shoulders. "Not that you've exactly left me a way of escape."

"What's going on, Kate? First you leave me at the restaurant, and now you make a quick exit on Devan Davis."

The sharp way he pronounced the man's name was enough to clue Kate in on his opinion of Devan. She was glad Todd didn't like him, and a sharp stab of guilt assailed her at the thought.

She was no better. In fact, she was worse. Much worse. When Todd opened the door tonight and she realized that Devan Davis, of all people, was standing on the other side, she'd been as close to fainting as she'd ever been in her life—and she didn't believe in fainting.

It had never occurred to her to ask her mother who was buying the house. Truth be told, she didn't want to know. A sad case of denial, she now realized, and foolish as well. If she'd known, she could have prepared, though she wasn't certain anything could prepare her for the shock of seeing Devan face-to-face after all these years.

That the man could move into her home just galled her.

Not that there was a thing she could do about it, she thought bitterly.

When he'd first walked through the door, she steeled herself for the meeting, Devan or no Devan. A couple of hours, tops, and the closing would be complete. And she was suddenly finding it easy to consider moving far away from here long before Devan moved in. If she saw him again in this lifetime, it would be too soon.

And then he had to go and look at her like she was a piece of meat he was about to devour. Even now, after splashing cold water on her face, the thought made her stomach churn. How could he look at her like...like *that?*

How dare he? And the fact that he now looked at her with interest made not one iota of difference. If anything, it made things worse. She would never, never forget the mocking look in his eyes when he yanked her around the dance floor, making fun of her weight.

Her humiliation at his hands was unforgivable. And that was why she'd excused herself. The urge to slap him in the face was stronger than she could control. She supposed there was some poetic justice in the fact that Devan had turned into a chubby, balding, desk-chair type of man who looked ten years older than he really was.

She needed to pray, really pray and ask God's forgiveness for her attitude. That was what she was doing when Todd had knocked. Now, he was waiting for an explanation, and she had none to give.

He eyed her speculatively, then reached out and brushed a lock of hair away from her face. The movement was so tender that her heart welled with love. Despite everything, even what she'd pulled with him in the restaurant, he still cared.

And she knew she owed him an explanation. The whole

truth this time, ugly warts and all. He deserved no less for the way he stood by her both in bad times and in good.

"About the restaurant…" she began, not really knowing how to put into words what had happened to her. "And Devan. It all has to do with the same incident."

He nodded. "Go on."

"I was in high school at the time. Ninth grade. I was…" she choked on the word, "overweight. No. I was downright fat."

"Kate, I don't—"

"No, no," she said, holding up a hand. "Don't interrupt. This is my story to tell."

He clamped his jaw shut and nodded, his brow furrowed, his gaze full of concern.

"Needless to say, I wasn't very popular. But like all young teens, I wanted to be. Desperately. So when I found out I'd been nominated for homecoming queen, I thought all my dreams had come true."

She stopped and took a deep breath, remembering.

"Mom helped me prepare. She even splurged and bought me a new dress. I still remember practicing a slow song with Daddy so I wouldn't mess up in front of the whole school." She laughed bitterly. "I convinced myself they liked me."

Todd reached for her hand, but she brushed it away, afraid his touch might set off deeper emotions than she could handle at the moment. She didn't need her internal sprinkler system setting off. Todd had seen enough immature behavior from her for one lifetime.

He crossed his arms over his chest and frowned.

"It was all a joke, you see. The popular kids had gotten together and decided to make a spectacle of me. And I wanted it so bad I walked right into their trap. In a sense, it really was my own fault."

Todd shook his head, his fists clenching. Kate reached out a hand, brushing it over his fists so he would relax.

"What happened?" he asked, his voice coarse.

"I went to the dance and was crowned homecoming queen. I still remember the joy I felt at that moment, especially when Devan Davis was crowned king. I had a crush on him."

Todd's fists clenched again, and she could see his pulse beating rapidly in the corner of his jaw.

"Traditionally, the king and queen were supposed to share a dance. A slow song. Instead, Devan grabbed my arm and paraded me around, letting the whole school jeer at me. I felt like such a fool. You know how tender the teenage psyche is."

"I'm going to go in there and—"

"And do what, Todd? Give him a broken nose? Ten minutes ago I wanted you to, you know. But God's been convicting me. I've been wearing this bitterness on my shoulder for too long. It's time I let go and move on. I think that's why Devan's here tonight." She paused and laughed. "Of course, he's also here to buy my house."

Todd reached out his arms, and this time Kate didn't back away. He held her lightly, rubbing up and down her back with the tips of his fingers.

"I haven't danced with anyone since that night," she whispered, leaning into his chest.

He held her away from him, understanding lighting his eyes. "That's why you ran away."

"Yes. A poor excuse at best. But it's just as well it happened. You deserve a lot better than me."

Todd's grip tightened on her shoulders. "What's that supposed to mean?"

The vehemence in his words surprised her. Angry sparks

flew from his eyes as their gazes met and locked. He probed, looking deep into her soul.

"Just what I said. You deserve better. You're such a gentleman. You're kind, gentle, handsome, and most of all, you've got a heart for God unlike any man I've ever met. Those are special qualities, worthy of a special woman."

His face flushed with anger and his fingers quivered. Kate had the unsettling notion he wanted to wrap his hands around her neck and strangle the living daylights out of her.

Instead, he turned her by the shoulders so she could look in the full-length mirror on the wall. "Kate, what do you see when you look in the mirror?"

"M-o-o-o-o-o-o-o," she answered promptly, chuckling at her own joke.

His brow furrowed. "Be serious. What do you see?"

Anger swelled in her chest, making her heartbeat increase. "I am being serious. That's what I see in the mirror, Todd. A big, fat, ugly cow."

He made a scratchy sound deep in his throat and turned her toward him. His eyes were flashing fire. His gaze dropped to her lips, then moved back up to her eyes. A determined look replaced the anger. Determination and...something else she couldn't place.

His hands slid from her shoulders to cup her face in his palms. Before she could fathom his intentions, he was kissing her.

In all the times she'd dreamed of this very moment, she'd never imagined it would be like this. Instead of the soft, gentle kiss of her dreams, Todd was kissing her hard, demanding a response, searing her with his lips and with his soul. Every ounce of passion he put into his life was in this kiss, and it sent Kate reeling.

She couldn't move, breathe, or think. All she could do was feel.

And then it was over, as abruptly as it had started. Her lips felt vacant without the pleasant pressure of Todd's mouth on hers, and her head was spinning.

He turned her back to the mirror. "What do you see?" he asked again, his voice raspy.

She pulled in a ragged breath. "I see..." she stared hard into the mirror, wondering what he expected. Wondering if he would kiss her again. "I don't know. Pudgy face, impossibly straight hair—"

He cut her off again, kissing her every bit as passionately as the last time. The smell of his sea-fresh aftershave assailed her nostrils, and she breathed deeply. His lips were still hard on hers, sending shocks of electricity clear to her toes.

Then he stepped back and turned her once again toward the mirror. "What do you see?" His voice was no more than a hoarse whisper.

She sighed and looked again, wondering if he planned to keep this up all night. "I don't know! What is it you want me to see?" All she could see was plain old Kate Logan staring back at her. What did he expect her to see? Cinderella?

He turned her toward him once again, and she braced herself for another heated kiss. This time though, he just cupped her face in his hands and stared deeply into her eyes.

Finally, with infinite slowness, he inched forward, brushing his lips across hers so lightly and gently it took her breath away. She didn't know how much time had passed when at last he lifted his head. "Now," he said, the corner of his mouth tipping up, "look in the mirror and tell me what you see, Kate Logan."

She turned toward the mirror, not expecting to see anything different from before. But it was there. A gentle, subtle difference in her.

It could be the delicate, rosy flush to her cheeks and lips brought about by his kisses. It could be the love shining brightly from her eyes. But it seemed to go deeper than that, right to her soul.

She saw a woman in love.

A smile started deep in her heart and moved to her lips.

Dearly beloved. Maybe whoever wrote "love conquers all" wasn't so very far off. What she saw was the result of *being* loved. Unconditionally. Faults and all. She met Todd's gaze in the mirror's reflection, and she could see he knew her thoughts.

"Back on the playing field," he said slowly, wrapping his arms around her waist, "I reminded you that Jesus loved you." He chuckled and tightened his hold on her. "Afterward, I thought I was the biggest idiot who'd ever lived, citing some children's Bible song to you."

"But that's the crux of it, isn't it?" she asked, smiling.

"It is," he agreed, his voice rich and deep. "And there's more."

"Yes?" she said, her breath catching in her throat. "What else could there be?"

"Jesus loves you," he repeated, nuzzling her neck. "And I love you too."

He released her and stuffed a hand into the inside pocket of his sport coat, withdrawing a small, black velvet box. Clearing his throat, he dropped to one knee and took her hand.

Her heart soared at the look of love in his eyes. Love! For her!

"Kate Whatever-Your-Middle-Name-Is Logan…" he began, then paused and licked his lips. "What is your full name, anyway?"

"Katrina Marie Logan," she choked out. Her hand was beginning to quiver in his.

"Nice name." His voice dropped an octave. "Katrina Marie Logan, will you please put me out of my misery and say you'll be my wife?"

Heedless of her guests, who were by this time no doubt wondering where they'd run off to, Kate shouted for joy.

"Does this mean yes?" he asked, rising to his feet and wrapping his arms around her for another kiss.

"Yes. A million times over, yes!"

"Good," he said, and kissed her soundly. Again and again, until Kate was certain the mirrors were steaming up.

"Devan's still in the kitchen!" she suddenly cried, jumping away from Todd and laughing nervously. "I'm supposed to be closing on this house!"

"Speaking of the house," he said, unlocking the bathroom door, "I have a suggestion about where you could move. Your favorite neighborhood, as I recall. And this particular townhouse especially needs your woman's touch. Providing, of course, that you can use all that wedding consulting knowledge to put your own wedding together in record time. Now that I have you, I don't want to waste a single moment."

"Me neither! Oh!" she exclaimed suddenly, getting excited all over again. "But what about your sister? Doesn't she live with you?"

"Moves out next week. And Kate," he added, "we have her blessing. And your mother's. Oh—and Thomas and Elizabeth wish us the best, too!"

"So that's why you didn't call me today!"

"That and I was getting cauliflower ear from listening to your phone ring and ring with no answer."

She threw him an apologetic glance. "I love you, Todd Andrew Jensen."

He smiled and took her hand. "I love you, too, Kate Logan. Now, should we go explain to your guests why we took so long?"

Kate was no longer afraid. Her hands were trembling, but with joy, not anxiety. She flushed a little when they returned to the kitchen, but only for a moment.

"Where did you two scamper off to?" her mother asked, her eyes gleaming.

"I…er…the bathroom," said Kate, clearing her throat.

"Longest bathroom break in history," said Todd, and everyone broke into laughter.

"Your timing is impeccable," her mother continued. "I've already signed the papers, so all you have to do is smile and wish the new owners well."

"The smiling part will be easy," Todd quipped.

"So I see," Elise replied. "You look like the cat that ate the canary, young man."

"As well I should." He took Kate's hand and laced his fingers through hers. "Wish me happy. You're soon going to be my mother."

Elise jumped up and hugged them both, exclaiming her joy. "Oh, thank God. Thank God." She pinched Todd's cheek as a grandmother would a toddler. "You'll be a blessing to this household. And I'm sure I'll be cuddling grandbabies before long."

"I hope so, ma'am."

"Mom, you mean," she corrected.

"Mom."

Kate couldn't speak. She tried, but the lump in her throat was cutting off her breath. Her head was spinning with delirious happiness, and she hugged her mother tight.

"See, I told you," Elise whispered for Kate's ears only. "Everything worked out in the end."

"Better than I could ever have dreamed," she agreed, her voice tight with emotion.

"God's way always is."

Devan stood and cleared his throat. "Congratulations, Kate." He held out his hand.

She stared at it in bemused silence for a moment, then smiled into his eyes. There was no animosity lurking in the back of her heart anymore. Happiness had invaded every corner of her being, wiping out all traces of lingering bitterness. "Thanks, Devan. I wish you well in your new house. I'm sure you'll enjoy living here."

It surprised her that she meant what she said. She no longer regretted the sale of the house, not with Todd's smile beaming rays of love at her. She was ready for some sunshine, and the future looked bright.

Epilogue

K ate walked down the aisle, vaguely aware of the red carpet unrolled over the sawdust at her feet. The small chapel was full to bursting, and everyone was there to see her.

Her tea-length white satin gown swirled around her knees, just like in the fairy tales. For a moment, she considered twirling just to see the fabric spin, but, of course, she resisted the impulse and bit back a smile.

Every eye was upon her. The wedding march was playing, and her time had come. At her side Thomas smiled and offered his arm. In lieu of her father, she'd chosen her dear friend to escort her to her soon-to-be husband.

She thought she'd be nervous and, indeed, felt the smallest twinge when everyone turned in unison to see her approach. But then she caught Todd's eye, and she was nervous no more.

He stood front and center, handsome in a black tuxedo and black-and-white striped ascot, his brown eyes wide with admiration as he took in his bride. A more dashing, handsome groom she couldn't imagine.

How could she be nervous, with dear Todd waiting for her? Her only obstacle was not dashing up the aisle just to be in his arms.

She coached herself mentally, just as she'd done with her clients a hundred times. *Step, pause. Step, pause.* Create a rhythm in your mind. *Step, pause. Step, pause.*

She slid a smile toward her mother as she walked past. Elise was positively glowing with excitement. No doubt picturing hoards of grandchildren brightening her future.

Elizabeth stood at the front, clasping her hands together and looking as nervous as Kate felt. Tears of joy streamed down her face, and when Kate met her gaze, she laughed in delight.

Tam waved and blew her a kiss from where she stood on the groom's side. Kate smiled. It would be nice to have a sister.

And then she was by Todd's side, and all she could think of was him. Elizabeth stepped forward to take her bouquet, smiling in her happiness. Todd took Kate's hand, and they turned to the chaplain, a friend of Todd from his seminary days.

He smiled and nodded his head, first at Todd, and then at Kate. Love welled inside her heart as she schooled her mind to heed the chaplain's words.

"Dearly beloved in the Lord." He gestured with his arm to include their guests.

"We are gathered together here in the sight of God, and in the face of this company, to join together this man and this woman...."

Dear Reader,

It's hard to believe this book has finally come to fruition. The glory belongs entirely to God, with a big thank-you to my husband, Joe, for helping me comprehend the wonderful, fine line between faith and works.

Like Kate in this story, I've struggled with self-esteem and self-doubt. I knew that if I delighted in God, he would give me the desire of my heart, but my faith stopped at praying. It was Joe who loved me enough to tell me I should be writing instead of dreaming.

I think low self-esteem is especially prevalent in women. Sometimes, as in *Beloved*, the love of a godly man can make all the difference in the world. I know that's how it was with me. But we don't need anyone, man or woman, to find our self-worth. We find self-worth only in the cross of our Lord Jesus Christ.

He loved you enough to die for you, to give himself in your place. It is here, my friend, that you can find truth, hope, and most of all, love. You are indeed his beloved.

Blessings,

Deb Kastner

Write to Debra Kastner
c/o Palisades
P.O. Box 1720
Sisters, Oregon 97759

THE PALISADES LINE

Look for these new releases at your local bookstore. If the title you seek is not in stock, the store may order you a copy using the ISBN listed.

Dalton's Dilemma, Lynn Bulock
ISBN 1-57673-238-X
Lacey Robbins, single mother of her sister's four children, is seeking adventure. But she never expected to find it by running into—literally!—handsome Jack Dalton at the roller rink. And she never expected the attraction between them to change her life forever....

Heartland Skies, Melody Carlson
ISBN 1-57673-264-9
Jayne Morgan moves to the small town of Paradise with the prospect of marriage, a new job, and plenty of horses to ride. But when her fiancé dumps her, she's left with loose ends. Then she wins a horse in a raffle, and the handsome rancher who boards her horse makes things look decidedly better.

Shades of Light, Melody Carlson (August 1998)
ISBN 1-57673-283-5
When widow Gwen Sullivan's daughter leaves for college, she discovers she can't bear her empty nest and takes a job at an interior decorating firm. But tedious work and a fussy boss leave her wondering if she's made the right move. Then Oliver Black, a prominent businessman, solicits her services and changes her mind....

Memories, Peggy Darty
ISBN 1-57673-171-5
In this sequel to *Promises,* Elizabeth Calloway is left with amnesia after witnessing a hit-and-run accident. Her husband, Michael, takes her on a vacation to Cancún so that she can relax and recover her memory. What they don't realize is that a killer is following them, hoping to wipe out Elizabeth's memory permanently....

Spirits, Peggy Darty (October 1998)
ISBN 1-57673-304-1
Picking up where *Memories* left off, the Calloways take a vacation to Angel Valley to find a missing woman. They enlist the help of a local writer who is an expert in Smoky Mountain legend and uncover a strange web of folklore and spirits.

Remembering the Roses, Marion Duckworth
ISBN 1-57673-236-3
Sammie Sternberg is trying to escape her memories of the man who betrayed her and ends up in a small town on the Olympic Peninsula in Washington. There she opens her dream business—an antique shop in an old Victorian—and meets a reclusive watercolor artist who helps to heal her broken heart.

Waterfalls, Robin Jones Gunn
ISBN 1-57673-221-5
In a visit to Glenbrooke, Oregon, Meredith Graham meets movie star Jacob Wilde and is sure he's the one. But when Meri puts her foot in her mouth, things fall apart. Is isn't until the two of them get thrown together working on a book-and-movie project that Jacob realizes his true feelings, and this time he's the one who's starstruck.

China Doll, Barbara Jean Hicks
ISBN 1-57673-262-2
Bronson Bailey is having a mid-life crisis: after years of globe-trotting in his journalism career, he's feeling restless. Georgine Nichols has also reached a turning point: after years of longing for a child, she's decided to adopt. The problem is, now she's fallen in love with Bronson, and he doesn't want a child.

Angel in the Senate, Kristen Johnson Ingram
ISBN 1-57673-263-0
Newly elected senator Megan Likely heads to Washington with high hopes for making a difference in government. But accusations of election fraud, two shocking murders, and threats on her life make the Senate take a back seat. She needs to find answers, but she's not sure who she can trust anymore.

Irish Rogue, Annie Jones
ISBN 1-57673-189-8
Michael Shaughnessy has paid the price for stealing a pot of gold, and now he's ready to make amends to the people he's hurt. Fiona O'Dea is number one on his list. The problem is, Fiona doesn't want to let Michael near enough to hurt her again. But before she knows it, he's taken his Irish charm and worked his way back into her life...and her heart.

Beloved, Debra Kastner
ISBN 1-57673-331-9
Wanted: A part-time pastor with a full-time heart for a wedding ministry. When wedding coordinator Kate Logan places the ad for a pastor, she doesn't expect a man like Todd Jensen to apply. But she quickly learns that he's perfect for the job—and perfect for her heart.

On Assignment, Marilyn Kok
ISBN 1-57673-279-7
When photographer Tessa Brooks arrives in Singapore for an assignment, she's both excited and nervous about seeing her ex-fiancé, banker Michael Lawton. Michael has mixed feelings, too: he knows he still loves Tessa, but will he ever convince her that they can get past the obstacle of their careers and make their relationship work?

Forgotten, Lorena McCourtney
ISBN 1-57673-222-3
A woman wakes up in an Oregon hospital with no memory of who she is. When she's identified as Kat Cavanaugh, she returns to her home in California. As Kat struggles to recover her memory, she meets a fiancé she doesn't trust and an attractive neighbor who can't believe how she's changed. She begins to wonder if she's really Kat Cavanaugh, but if she isn't, what happened to the real Kat?

Canyon, Lorena McCourtney (September 1998)
ISBN 1-57673-287-8
Kit Holloway and Tyler McCord are wildly in love, planning their wedding, and looking forward to a summer of white-water rafting through the Grand Canyon. Then the actions of two people they love rip apart their relationship. Can their love survive, or will their differences prove to be too much?

Rustlers, Karen Rispin (September 1998)
ISBN 1-57673-292-4
Amber Lacey is on the run—from her home, from her career, and from God. She ends up working on a ranch in western

Alberta and trying to keep the secrets of her past from the man she's falling in love with. But then sinister dealings on the ranch force Amber to confront the mistakes she's made—and turn back to the God who never gave up on her.

The Key, Gayle Roper
ISBN 1-57673-223-1
On Kristie Matthews's first day living on an Amish farm, she gets bitten by a dog and is rushed to the emergency room by a handsome stranger. In the ER, an elderly man in the throes of a heart attack hands her a key and tells her to keep it safe. Suddenly odd accidents begin to happen to her, but no one's giving her any answers.

The Document, Gayle Roper (October 1998)
ISBN 1-57673-295-9
While Cara Bentley is sorting through things after the death of her grandfather, she stumbles upon evidence that he was adopted. Determined to find her roots, she heads to Lancaster County and settles in at an Amish farm. She wants to find out who she is, but she can't help wondering: if it weren't for the money in John Bentley's will, would anyone else care about her identity?

ANTHOLOGIES

Fools for Love, Ball, Brooks, Jones
ISBN 1-57673-235-5
By Karen Ball: Kitty starts pet-sitting, but when her clients turn out to be more than she can handle, she enlists help from a handsome handyman.

By Jennifer Brooks: Caleb Murphy tries to acquire a book collection from a widow, but she has one condition: he must marry her granddaughter first.

By Annie Jones: A college professor who has been burned by love vows not to be fooled twice, until her ex-fiancé shows up and ruins her plans!

Heart's Delight, Ball, Hicks, Noble
ISBN 1-57673-220-7

By Karen Ball: Corie receives a Valentine's Day date from her sisters and thinks she's finally found the one…until she learns she went out with the wrong man.

By Barbara Jean Hicks: Carina and Reid are determined to break up their parents' romance, but when it looks like things are working, they have a change of heart.

By Diane Noble: Two elderly bird-watchers set aside their differences to try to save a park from disaster, but learn they've bitten off more than they can chew.

Be sure to look for any of the 1997 titles you may have missed:

Surrender, Lynn Bulock (ISBN 1-57673-104-9)
Single mom Cassie Neel accepts a blind date from her children for her birthday.

Wise Man's House, Melody Carlson (ISBN 1-57673-070-0)
A young widow buys her childhood dream house, and a mysterious stranger moves into her caretaker's cottage.

Moonglow, Peggy Darty (ISBN 1-57673-112-X)
Tracy Kosell comes back to Moonglow, Georgia, and investigates a case with a former schoolmate, who's now a detective.

Promises, Peggy Darty (ISBN 1-57673-149-9)
A Christian psychologist asks her detective husband to help her find a dangerous woman.

Texas Tender, Sharon Gillenwater (ISBN 1-57673-111-1)
Shelby Nolan inherits a watermelon farm and asks the sheriff for help when two elderly men begin digging holes in her fields.

Clouds, Robin Jones Gunn (ISBN 1-57673-113-8)
Flight attendant Shelly Graham runs into her old boyfriend, Jonathan Renfield, and learns he's engaged.

Sunsets, Robin Jones Gunn (ISBN 1-57673-103-0)
Alissa Benson has a run-in at work with Brad Phillips, and is more than a little upset when she finds out he's her neighbor!

Snow Swan, Barbara Jean Hicks (ISBN 1-57673-107-3)
Toni, an unwed mother and a recovering alcoholic, falls in love for the first time. But if Clark finds out the truth about her past, will he still love her?

Irish Eyes, Annie Jones (ISBN 1-57673-108-1)
Julia Reed gets drawn into a crime involving a pot of gold and has her life turned upside-down by Interpol agent Cameron O'Dea.

Father by Faith, Annie Jones (ISBN 1-57673-117-0)
Nina Jackson buys a dude ranch and hires cowboy Clint Cooper as her foreman, but her son, Alex, thinks Clint is his new daddy!

Stardust, Shari MacDonald (ISBN 1-57673-109-X)
Gillian Spencer gets her dream assignment but is shocked to learn she must work with Maxwell Bishop, who once broke her heart.

Kingdom Come, Amanda MacLean (ISBN 1-57673-120-0)
Ivy Rose Clayborne, M.D., pairs up with the grandson of the coal baron to fight the mining company that is ravaging her town.

Dear Silver, Lorena McCourtney (ISBN 1-57673-110-3)
When Silver Sinclair receives a letter from Chris Bentley ending their relationship, she's shocked, since she's never met the man!

Enough! Gayle Roper (ISBN 1-57673-185-5)
When Molly Gregory gets fed up with her three teenaged children, she announces that she's going on strike.

A Mother's Love, Bergren, Colson, MacLean (ISBN 1-57673-106-5)
Three heartwarming stories share the joy of a mother's love.

Silver Bells, Bergren, Krause, MacDonald (ISBN 1-57673-119-7)
Three novellas focus on romance during Christmastime.